Table of Contents

Soft Evening Shawl,
page 10

2 Rose Leaf Top

5 Luscious Lace Scarf

8 Evening Clutch

10 Soft Evening Shawl

15 Delicate Lace Shawl

20 Lovely Lace Table Set

23 Pineapple & Diamonds Table Runner

26 Easy Lace Coasters

28 Pineapple Coaster

30 Simple Table Runner

32 Lacy Bread Basket Cover

34 Lacy Bookmark Trio

38 Lace Star Candle Mat

40 Pineapple Lap Throw

44 Beaded Lace Lampshade

Pineapple Lap Throw,
page 40

Luscious Lace Scarf,
page 5

Meet The Designer

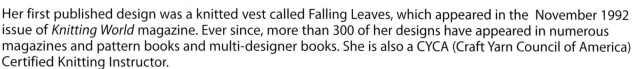

Nazanin S. Fard has been knitting since age four. She learned to crochet in middle school. In 1980, she received her Bachelor of Science degree in Computer Science, and worked as a computer programmer for eight years.

Her first published design was a knitted vest called Falling Leaves, which appeared in the November 1992 issue of *Knitting World* magazine. Ever since, more than 300 of her designs have appeared in numerous magazines and pattern books and multi-designer books. She is also a CYCA (Craft Yarn Council of America) Certified Knitting Instructor.

In 2003, she co-founded the Needlecraft University (www.NeedlecraftUniversity.com) which is an online facility for teaching classes in knitting, crochet and silk ribbon embroidery. Since 2007, she has offered her patterns through an online PDF magazine found at www.craftland.com/lacenmore.

Rose Leaf Top

Design by Nazanin Fard

Skill Level

⬤⬤⬤⬜ EXPERIENCED

Sizes

Women's small (medium, large, X-large) Instructions are given for smallest size with larger sizes in parentheses. When only 1 number is given it applies to all sizes.

Finished Measurements

Bust: 36 (40, 44, 48) inches
Total length: 25 inches
Armhole depth: 8 (8, 8½, 8½) inches
Sleeve length to underarm: 20 inches

Materials

- NaturallyCaron.com Country 75% microdenier acrylic/25% merino wool worsted weight yarn (185 yds/85g per ball): 7 (8, 9, 10) balls green sheen #0004
- Size 6 (4mm) 24-inch circular needle
- Size 7 (4.5mm) needles or size needed to obtain gauge
- Yarn needle

4 MEDIUM

Gauge

Two reps of Double Rose Leaf pat = 5 inches with larger needles.
To save time, take time to check gauge.

Special Abbreviations

Slip, slip, knit (ssk): Slip next 2 sts one at a time as if to knit, insert LH needle into fronts of 2 slipped sts and k2tog from this position to dec 1 st.

Slip, knit 2 together, pass (sk2p): Slip next st, k2tog, pass slipped st over knit st and off needle to dec 2 sts.

Pattern Stitches

Double Rose Leaf (multiple of 16 sts + 1)

Note: The pattern multiple is reduced from 16 to 14 sts on Row 2; original multiple is restored on Row 8.

Row 1 (WS): Purl across.

Row 2: *K1, yo, k1, ssk, p1, k2tog, k1, p1, k1, ssk, p1, k2tog, k1, yo; rep from * across to last st, k1.

Row 3 and all odd numbered rows: Knit the knits and purl the purls and yarn overs.

Row 4: *[K1, yo] twice, ssk, p1, k2tog, p1, ssk, p1, k2tog, yo, k1, yo; rep from * to last st, k1.

Row 6: *K1, yo, k3, yo, sk2p, p1, k3tog, yo, k3, yo; repeat from * to last st, k1.

Row 8: *K1, yo, k5, yo, sk2p, yo, k5, yo; rep from * to last st, k1.

Rep Rows 1–8 for pat.

Lace Rib (multiple of 4 sts + 2)

Row 1 (WS): K2, *p2, k2; rep from * across.

Row 2: *P2, k2tog, yo; rep from * to last 2 sts, p2.

Row 3: Rep Row 1.

Row 4: *P2, yo, ssk; rep from * to last 2 sts, p2.

Rep Rows 1–4 for pat.

Pattern Notes

Charts are included for Double Rose Leaf and Lace Rib patterns for those preferring to work pattern stitches from a chart.
On these charts odd-numbered rows are wrong side rows and are worked from left to right across the chart; even-numbered rows are right side rows and are worked from right to left across the chart.

Back

With larger needle, cast on 113 (129, 145, 161) sts.

Knit 3 rows.

Work Rows 1–8 of Double Rose Leaf pat for 7 inches.

Next row: Knit, dec 3 sts evenly spaced across row—110 (126, 142, 158) sts.

Work in Lace Rib pat until piece measures 17 (17, 16½, 16½) inches from cast-on edge.

Shape armhole

Bind off 4 (4, 5, 5) sts at the beg of next 2 rows—102 (118, 132, 148) sts.

Dec 1 st each end [every other row] 6 times—90 (106, 120, 136) sts.

Continue even in Lace Rib pat as established until piece measures 23 inches.

Shape neck
Work in pat as established over next 27 (35, 40, 45) sts; attach another ball of yarn and bind off center 36 (36, 40, 46) sts, work in pat across rem sts.

Working both sides at once in pat as established, dec 1 st at neck edge [every other row] 3 times—24 (32, 37, 42) sts on each shoulder.

Shape shoulder
Bind off 8 (10, 12, 14) sts at armhole edge [every other row] twice—8 (12, 13, 14) sts on each shoulder.

Bind off rem sts.

Front
Work same as back until piece measures 19 inches.

Shape neck
Work across 40 (45, 50, 55) sts in pat as established, attach another ball of yarn and bind off 10 (16, 20, 26) center sts, work in pat across rem sts.

Working both sides at once in pat as established bind off 4 (3, 3, 3) sts at neck edge [every other row] 3 times—28 (36, 41, 46) sts on each shoulder.

Dec 1 st at neck edge [every other row] 4 times—24 (32, 37, 42) sts on each shoulder.

Shape shoulder
Bind off 8 (10, 12, 14) sts at armhole edge [every other row] twice—8 (12, 13, 14) sts on each shoulder.

Bind off rem sts.

Sleeve
Make 2

With larger needle, cast on 97 sts.

Knit 3 rows.

Work [Rows 1–8 of Double Rose Leaf pat] 4 times.

Next row (RS): Dec 47 (43, 39, 35) sts evenly spaced across row—50 (54, 58, 62) sts.

Work in Lace Rib pat inc 1 st each edge [every 6 rows] 13 times, working inc sts into pat—76 (80, 84, 88) sts.

Work even in pat as established until piece measures 20 inches. Bind off 4 (4, 5, 5) sts at the beg of next 2 rows—68 (72, 74, 78) sts.

Dec 1 st each edge [every other row] 20 times—28 (32, 34, 38) sts.

Bind off 2 sts at the beg of next 4 rows—20 (24, 26, 30) sts.

Sizes large and X-large only: Bind off 3 sts at the beg of next 2 rows—20 (24) sts.

Bind off all sts loosely.

Assembly
Sew shoulder seams.

Neck edging
With smaller circular needle, pick up and knit 124 (130, 138, 150) sts around the neck. Join and work in k1, p1 rib for 10 rnds.

Purl 2 rnds.

Bind off loosely.

Finishing
Sew sleeves in place, then sew sleeve and side seams. ❖

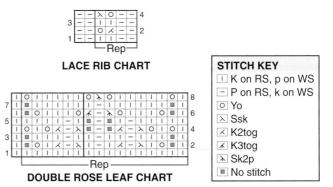

LACE RIB CHART

DOUBLE ROSE LEAF CHART

STITCH KEY
I	K on RS, p on WS
–	P on RS, k on WS
O	Yo
⅄	Ssk
⋌	K2tog
⋏	K3tog
⅄	Sk2p
■	No stitch

Luscious Lace Scarf

Design by Nazanin Fard

Skill Level

◼◼◼◻ EXPERIENCED

Finished Size

Approx 8 x 80 inches

Materials

- Conjoined Creations Pastimes, Too 100% soysilk laceweight yarn (480 yds/50g per skein): 1 skein terracotta
- Size 5 (3.75mm) knitting needles

Stitch Gauge

Gauge is not critical to this project.

Special Abbreviations

Slip, slip, knit (ssk): Slip next 2 sts one at a time as if to knit, insert LH needle into front of 2 slipped sts and k2tog from this position to dec 1 st.

Slip 2, knit 1, pass 2 over (sl2kp2sso): Slip next 2 sts, k1, pass 2 slipped sts over knit st and off needle to dec 2 sts.

Slip, knit 2 together, pass (sk2p): Slip next st, k2tog, pass slipped st over knit st and off needle to dec 2 sts.

Pattern Stitches

Triple Leaf Pattern (multiple of 14 sts +1)

Note: St count changes throughout the pat so sts should only be counted on Rows 2, 4 and 12 only.

Row 1 and all odd numbered rows: Purl across.

Row 2 (RS): *K1, yo, k2tog, k3tog, [yo, k1] 3 times, yo, k3tog-tbl, ssk, yo; rep from * to last st, k1.

Row 4: *K1, yo, k3tog, yo, k7, yo, k3tog-tbl, yo; rep from * to last st, k1.

Row 6: *K1, yo, k2tog, yo, k1, yo, k2, sl2kp2sso, k2, yo, k1, yo, ssk, yo; rep from * to last st, k1.

Row 8: *K1, yo, k2tog, yo, k3, yo, k1, sl2kp2sso, k1, yo, k3, yo, ssk, yo; rep from * to last st, k1.

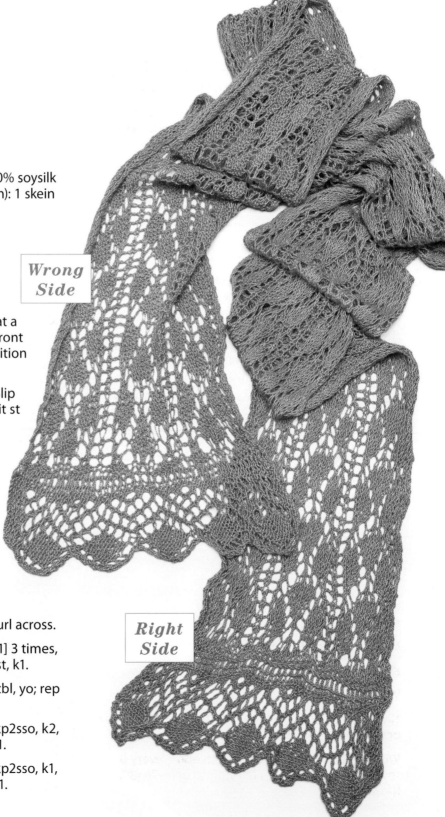

Wrong Side

Right Side

House of White Birches, Berne, Indiana 46711 DRGnetwork.com

Row 10: *K1, yo, [k2tog] twice, k3, yo, sl2kp2sso, yo, k3, [ssk] twice, yo; rep from * to last st, k1.

Row 12: *K1, yo, [k2tog] 3 times, [k1, yo] twice, k1, [ssk] 3 times, yo; rep from * to last st, k1.

Rep Rows 1–12 for pat.

Edging (worked over 12 sts)

Row 1 (RS): K11, ssk (1 st from edging and 1 st from scarf).

Row 2: Sl 1p, purl across.

Row 3: Sl 1p, k1-tbl, yo, k1, [yo, ssk] 3 times, k2, ssk (1 st from edging and 1 st from scarf).

Row 4 and all even numbered rows: Sl 1p, purl across.

Row 5: Sl 1p, k1-tbl, yo, k3, [yo, ssk] 3 times, k1, ssk (1 st from edging and 1 st from scarf).

Row 7: Sl 1p, k1-tbl, yo, k5, [yo, ssk] twice, k2, ssk (1 st from edging and 1 st from scarf).

Row 9: Sl 1p, k1-tbl, yo, k7, [yo, ssk] twice, k1, ssk (1 st from edging and 1 st from scarf).

Row 11: Ssk, k1, yo, ssk, k3, [k2tog, yo] twice, k3, ssk (1 st from edging and 1 st from scarf).

Row 13: Ssk, k1, yo, ssk, k1, [k2tog, yo] 3 times, k2, ssk (1 st from edging and 1 st from scarf).

Row 15: Ssk, k1, yo, sk2p, yo, [k2tog, yo] twice, k3, ssk (1 st from edging and 1 st from scarf).

Row 17: Ssk, k2, [k2tog, yo] 3 times, k2, ssk (1 st from edging and 1 st from scarf).

Row 18: Sl 1p, purl across.

Rep Rows 3–18 for pat.

Pattern Notes

Chart is provided for those preferring to work Triple Leaf and Edging pattern stitches from a chart.
Two stitches are worked at each end in garter stitch throughout body of scarf; these stitches are not included on the Triple Leaf chart.
Only right side rows are shown on the chart. Wrong side rows are worked slip 1 purlwise, purl across.

Scarf

Provisionally cast on 47 sts.

Knit 3 rows of garter st.

Keeping 2 sts at each edge in garter st and center 43 sts in Triple Leaf Pat work until scarf measures about 80 inches, ending by working Row 18.

Knit 2 rows of garter stitch. Do not bind off.

Cable cast on 12 sts and work in Edging pat until 1 st is left on the edge of the scarf.

Work Rows 1 and 2 of Edging.

Bind off all sts loosely.

Place all sts from cast-on edge of the scarf on the needle and work same as above for the other edge.

Weave in all ends.

Block scarf to size. ❖

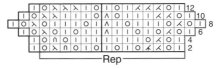

TRIPLE LEAF CHART
WS purl rows not shown on chart.
Two garter st edge sts are not included on chart.

EDGING CHART
WS rows not shown on chart are worked as follows: Sl 1p, purl across.

STITCH KEY
| K on RS, p on WS
O Yo
⟋ K2tog
⟍ Ssk
⟫ K3tog
⋂ K3tog-tbl
∧ Sl2kp2sso
• Sl 1
⅄ K1-tbl
⟋• Sk2p

Evening Clutch

Design by Nazanin Fard

Rows 3, 5 and 7: K2, *yo, k2, k2tog, ssk, k2, yo, k1; rep from * across to last st, k1.

Rows 4, 6 and 8: Purl across.

Rep [Rows 1–8] 7 times.

Bind off all sts loosely.

I-cord Handle
Leaving a 6-inch tail, cast 5 sts onto 1 double-point needle, *slide sts to the other end of needle, pulling yarn tightly across back knit across; rep from * until I-cord measures 16 inches or desired length.

Bind off all sts loosely, leaving a 6-inch tail. Cut yarn.

Finishing
Hold 2 side pieces with RS tog, sew sides and bottom edge tog; do not sew top 2 pat reps. Turn RS out.

Fold the fabric in half. Sew side seams; do not sew length of top 2 pat reps. Insert the lining into the knitted piece. Sew both tops of knitted pieces to the top edges of the lining.

Place glue along edge of the purse frame. Insert the top part of the piece into the frame, let dry. Rep for other side.

Using the 6-inch tail, attach the handle to the holes provided on the sides of the frame. ❖

Skill Level
 INTERMEDIATE

Finished Size
Approx 5½ x 7 inches

Materials
• Patons Brilliant 69% acrylic/19% nylon/12% polyester DK weight yarn (166 yds/50g per ball): 1 ball crystal cream #03008
• Size 6 (4mm) straight and 2 double-point needles or size needed to obtain gauge
• Blumethal Craft Creative Naturals handbag frame metal in gold color, 5½ x 3 inches
• 6½ x 15 inch piece of lining fabric
• Yarn needle
• Sewing needle and matching thread
• Low temp glue gun

Gauge
2 pat reps = 3 inches wide by 2 inches long.
To save time, take time to check gauge.

Pattern Note
Chart has been included for those preferring to work pattern from a chart.

Clutch

Side
Make 2

Cast on 39 sts.

Row 1 (RS): Purl across.

Row 2: Knit across.

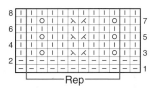

EVENING CLUTCH CHART

STITCH KEY
- ☐ K on RS, p on WS
- ☐ P on RS, k on WS
- ☐ Yo
- ☐ K2tog
- ☐ Ssk

Soft Evening Shawl

Design by Nazanin Fard

Skill Level

▰▰▰▱ EXPERIENCED

Finished Size

Top width: 54 inches
Each side: 39 inches
Gusset width: 5 inches

Materials

- Plymouth Baby Alpaca DK 100% baby alpaca DK weight yarn (125 yds/50g per ball): 8 balls dusty yellow #1104
- Size 6 (4mm) circular needle or size needed to obtain gauge
- Size F/5 (3.75mm) crochet hook
- Stitch markers
- Tapestry needle

3 LIGHT

Gauge

19 sts and 28 rows =4 inches/10 cm in St st.
To save time, take time to check gauge.

Special Abbreviations

Slip, slip, knit (ssk): Slip next 2 sts one at a time as if to knit, insert LH needle into fronts of 2 slipped sts and k2tog from this position to dec 1 st.

Slip, knit 2 together, pass (sk2p): Slip next st, k2tog, pass slipped st over knit st and off needle to dec 2 sts.

Pattern Notes

Charts are included for those preferring to work pattern from chart.

Rows 11–33 are shown on Chart A with instructions for repeats of those rows given in the written instructions. The 5 on each edge for border not shown on the chart are worked in garter stitch. Even-number rows not show are worked as: K5, purl to last 5 stitches, k5. Odd-number rows are worked from right to left from A to C, working repeats from B to C across to 3 stitches before the marker, then working the Gusset Chart, then working repeats from B to C with the last repeat ending at D.

Rows 113–150 are worked from written instructions.

Rows 151–165 are worked from Chart B. Even number rows not shown are worked as: K5, purl to last 5 sts, k5.

Shawl

Cast on 377 sts.

Row 1 (RS): K5, place marker, k172 for right side, place marker, k23 for gusset, place marker, k172 for left side, place marker, k5.

Rows 2–10: Knit across.

Row 11: For right side, K5, k2tog, *k1, [yo, ssk] twice, k2, [yo, ssk] twice, k3, [k2tog, yo] twice, k2, [k2tog, yo] twice*; rep from * to * to 3 sts to marker, k1, ssk; for gusset, [yo, ssk] twice, k2, [yo, ssk] twice, k3, [k2tog, yo] twice, k2, [k2tog, yo] twice; for left side k2tog, k1; rep from * to * to 3 sts before next marker, k1, ssk, k5.

Row 12 and all even numbered rows: K5, purl to last 5 sts, k5.

Row 13: For right side, k5, k2tog, k1, [yo, ssk] twice, k2, [yo, ssk] twice, k1, [k2tog, yo] twice, k2, [k2tog, yo] twice, k1, *k2, [yo, ssk] twice, k2, [yo, ssk] twice, k1, [k2tog, yo] twice, k2, [k2tog, yo] twice, k1*; rep from * to * to 3 sts before marker, k1, ssk; for gusset, k1, [yo, ssk] twice, k2, [yo, ssk] twice, k1, [k2tog, yo] twice, k2, [k2tog, yo] twice, k1; for left side, k2tog, k1; rep from * to * across to 2 sts before marker, ssk, k5.

Row 15: For right side, k5, k2tog, k1, [yo, ssk] twice, k2, yo, ssk, yo, sk2p, yo, k2tog, yo, k2, [k2tog, yo] twice, k2, *k3, [yo, ssk] twice, k2, yo, ssk, yo, sk2p, yo, k2tog, yo, k2, [k2tog, yo] twice, k2*; rep from * to * to 3 sts before marker, k1, ssk; for gusset, k2, [yo, ssk] twice, k2, yo, ssk, yo, sk2p, yo, k2tog, yo, k2, [k2tog, yo] twice, k2; for left side, k2tog, k1; rep from * to * across, ending last rep k1, ssk, k5.

Row 17: For right side, k5, k2tog, k1, [yo, ssk] twice, k2, yo, ssk, k1, k2tog, yo, k2, [k2tog, yo] twice, k3, *k4, [yo, ssk] twice, k2, yo, ssk, k1, k2tog, yo, k2, [k2tog, yo] twice, k3*; rep from * to * to 3 sts before marker, k1, ssk; for gusset, k3, [yo, ssk] twice, k2, yo, ssk, k1, k2tog, yo, k2, [k2tog, yo] twice, k3; for left side, k2tog, k1; rep from * to * across, ending last rep with k1, ssk, k5.

Row 19: For right side, k5, k2tog, k1, [yo, ssk] twice, k2, yo, sk2p, yo, k2, [k2tog, yo] twice, k4, *k5, [yo, ssk] twice, k2, yo, sk2p, yo, k2, [k2tog, yo] twice, k4*; rep from * to * to 3 sts before marker, k1, ssk; for gusset, k4, [yo, ssk] twice, k2, yo, sk2p, yo, k2, [k2tog, yo] twice, k4; for left side, k2tog, k1; rep from * to * across, ending last rep k1, ssk, k5.

Row 21: For right side, k5, k2tog, k1, [yo, ssk] twice, k5, [k2tog, yo] twice, k5, *k6, [yo, ssk] twice, k5, [k2tog, yo] twice, k5*; rep from * to * to 3 sts before marker, k1, ssk; for gusset, k5, [yo, ssk] twice, k5, [k2tog, yo] twice, k5; for left side, k2tog, k1; rep from * to * across, ending last rep k1, ssk, k5.

Row 23: For right side, k5, k2tog, k1, [yo, ssk] twice, k3, [k2tog, yo] twice, k6, *k7, [yo, ssk] twice, k3, [k2tog, yo] twice, k6*; rep from * to * to 3 sts before marker, k1, ssk; for gusset, k6, [yo, ssk] twice, k3, [k2tog, yo] twice, k6; for left side, k2tog, k1; rep from * to * across, ending last rep k1, ssk, k5.

Row 25: For right side, k5, k2tog, k1, [yo, ssk] twice, k1, [k2tog, yo] twice, k7, *k8, [yo, ssk] twice, k1, [k2tog, yo] twice, k7*; rep from * to * to 3 sts before marker, k1, ssk; for gusset, k7, [yo, ssk] twice, k1, [k2tog, yo] twice, k7; for left side, k2tog, k1; rep from * to * across, ending last rep k1, ssk, k5.

Row 27: For right side, k5, k2tog, k1, yo, ssk, yo, sk2p, yo, k2tog, yo, k8, *k9, yo, ssk, yo, sk2p, yo, k2tog, yo, k8*; rep from * to * to 3 sts before marker, k1, ssk; for gusset, k8, yo, ssk, yo, sl1-k2tog-psso, yo, k2tog, yo, k8; for left side, k2tog, k1; rep from * to * across, ending last rep k1, ssk, k5.

Row 29: For right side, k5, k2tog, k1, yo, ssk, k1, k2tog, yo, k9, *k10, yo, ssk, k1, k2tog, yo, k9*; rep from * to * to 3 sts before marker, k1, ssk; for gusset, k9, yo, ssk, k1, k2tog, yo, k9; for left side, k2tog, k1; rep from * to * across, ending last rep k1, ssk, k5.

Row 31: For right side, k5, k2tog, k1, yo, sk2p, yo, k10, *k11, yo, sk2p, yo, k10*; rep from * to * to 3 sts before marker, k1, ssk; for gusset, k10, yo, sk2p, yo, k10; for left side, k2tog, k1; rep from * to * across, ending last rep k1, ssk, k5.

Row 33: K5, *k2tog, knit to 2 sts before marker, ssk*; for gusset, k23; rep from * to *, k5.

Row 34: K5, purl to last 5 sts, k5.

Rows 35–60: Rep [Rows 33 and 34] 18 times.

Rows 61–108: Rep Rows 11–60.

Rows 109–111: Rep Rows 11–13.

Row 112 and all even-numbered rows: K5, purl to last 5 sts, k5.

Row 113: For right side, k5, k2tog, k1, [yo, ssk] twice, k2, yo, ssk, yo, sk2p, yo, k2tog, yo, k2, [k2tog, yo] twice, k2, *k3, [yo, ssk] twice, k2, yo, ssk, yo, sk2p, yo, k2tog, yo, k2, [k2tog, yo] twice, k2*; rep from * to * to 3 sts before marker, k1, ssk; for gusset, k2tog, [yo, ssk] twice, k2, yo, ssk, yo, sk2p, yo, k2tog, yo, k2, [k2tog, yo] twice, ssk; for left side, k2tog, k1; rep from * to * across, ending last rep with k1 instead of k2, ssk, k5.

Row 115: For right side, k5, k2tog, k1, [yo, ssk] twice, k2, yo, ssk, k1, k2tog, yo, k2, [k2tog, yo] twice, k3, *k4, [yo, ssk] twice, k2, yo, ssk, k1, k2tog, yo, k2, [k2tog, yo] twice, k3*; rep from * to * to 3 sts before marker, k1, ssk; for gusset, k2, [yo, ssk] twice, k2, yo, ssk, k1, k2tog, yo, k2, [k2tog, yo] twice, k2; for left side, k2tog, k1; rep from * to * across ending last rep with k1 instead of k3, ssk, k5.

Row 117: For right side, k5, k2tog, k1, [yo, ssk] twice, k2, yo, sk2p, yo, k2, [k2tog, yo] twice, k4, *k5, [yo, ssk] twice, k2, yo, sk2p, yo, k2, [k2tog, yo] twice, k4*; rep from * to * to 3 sts before marker, k1, ssk; for gusset, k2tog, k1, [yo, ssk] twice, k2, yo, sk2p, yo, k2, [k2tog, yo] twice, k2, ssk; for left side, k2tog, k1; rep from * to * across, ending last rep with k1 instead of k4, ssk, k5.

Row 119: For right side, k5, k2tog, k1, [yo, ssk] twice, k5, [k2tog, yo] twice, k5, *k6, [yo, ssk] twice, k5, [k2tog, yo] twice, k5*; rep from * to * to 3 sts before marker, k1, ssk; for gusset, k3, [yo, ssk] twice, k5, [k2tog, yo] twice, k3; for left side, k2tog, k1; rep from * to * across, ending last rep with k1, instead of k5, ssk, k5.

Row 121: For right side, k5, k2tog, k1, [yo, ssk] twice, k3, [k2tog, yo] twice, k6, *k7, [yo, ssk] twice, k3, [k2tog, yo] twice, k6*; rep from * to * to 3 sts before marker, k1, ssk; for gusset, k2tog, k2, [yo, ssk] twice, k3, [k2tog, yo] twice, k2, ssk; for left side, k2tog, k1; rep from * to * across, ending last rep with k1, instead of k6, ssk, k5.

Row 123: For right side, k5, k2tog, k1, [yo, ssk] twice, k1, [k2tog, yo] twice, k7, *k8, [yo, ssk] twice, k1, [k2tog, yo] twice, k7*; rep from * to * to 3 sts before marker, k1, ssk; for gusset, k4, [yo, ssk] twice, k1, [k2tog, yo] twice, k4; for left side, k2tog, k1; rep from * to * across, ending last rep with k1, instead of k7, ssk, k5.

Row 125: For right side, k5, k2tog, k1, yo, ssk, yo, sk2p, yo, k2tog, yo, k8, *k9, yo, ssk, yo, sk2p, yo, k2tog, yo, k8*; rep from * to * to 3 sts before marker, k1, ssk; for gusset, k2tog, k3, yo, ssk, yo, sk2p, yo, k2tog, yo, k3, ssk; for left side, k2tog, k1; rep from * to * across, ending last rep with k1, instead of k8, ssk, k5.

Row 127: For right side, k5, k2tog, k1, yo, ssk, k1, k2tog, yo, k9, *k10, yo, ssk, k1, k2tog, yo, k9*; rep from * to * to 3 sts before marker, k1, ssk; for gusset, k5, yo, ssk, k1, k2tog, yo, k5; for left side; k2tog, k1; rep from * to * across, ending last rep with k1, instead of k9, ssk, k5.

Row 129: For right side, k5, k2tog, k1, yo, sk2p, yo, k10, *k11, yo, sk2p, yo, k10*; rep from * to * to 3 sts before marker, k1, ssk; for gusset, k2tog, k4, yo, sk2p, yo, k4, ssk; for left side, k2tog, k1; rep from * to * across, ending last rep with k1, instead of k10, ssk, k5—133 sts (5 border sts + 55 right side sts + 13 gusset sts + 55 left side sts + 5 border sts).

Rows 131, 133 and 135: K5, *k2tog, knit to 2 sts before marker*, ssk, k13; rep from * to *, k5—121 sts.

Row 137: K5, k2tog, [k4, ssk] 7 times, k3, ssk, k13, ssk, k3, [k2tog, k4] 7 times, k4, ssk, k5—103 sts.

Row 139: K5, k2tog, k36, k2tog, k13, ssk, k36, ssk, k5—99 sts.

Row 141: K5, [k2tog, k4] 6 times, ssk, k13, [ssk, k4] 6 times, ssk, k5—85 sts.

Row 143: K5, k2tog, k27, ssk, k13, k2tog, k27, ssk, k5—81 sts.

Row 145: K5, k2tog, k25, ssk, k13, k2tog, k25, ssk, k5—77 sts.

Row 147: K5, k2tog, k23, ssk, k13, k2tog, k23, ssk, k5—73 sts.

Row 149: K5, k2tog, k21, ssk, k13, k2tog, k21, ssk, k5—69 sts.

Remove markers before continuing.

Row 151: K5, [k2tog] 11 times, k15, [ssk] 11 times, k5—47 sts.

Row 153: K5, k2tog, k8, k2tog, ssk, k9, k2tog, ssk, k8, ssk, k5—41 sts.

Row 155: K5, k2tog, k6, k2tog, ssk, k7, k2tog, ssk, k6, ssk, k5—35 sts.

Row 157: K5, k2tog, k4, k2tog, ssk, k5, k2tog, k4, ssk, k5—28 sts.

Row 159: K5, k2tog, k2, k2tog, ssk, k3, k2tog, ssk, k2, ssk, k5—23 sts.

Row 161: K5, [k2tog] twice, ssk, k1, k2tog, [ssk] twice, k5—17 sts.

Row 163: K5, k2tog, sk2p, ssk, k5—13 sts.

Row 165: K5, sk2p, k5—11 sts.

Bind off all sts loosely.

Finishing

With tapestry needle, sew the 5 sts on both sides together. Weave in all ends. Block shawl to size.

Fringe

Referring to photo, attach fringe to the lower edge of the shawl. Cut strands of yarn, 8 inches long. Fold each strand in half. Insert crochet hook from back to front into each stitch of the cast-on edge. Catch the center fold with hook and pull through the stitch creating a loop. Pass the ends through the loop. Pull tightly.

Trim ends of the fringe to make an even edge. ❖

SOFT EVENING SHAWL CHART B

Note: Five stitches at each side worked in garter stitch are not included on chart.
Even number rows not included on chart are worked as: K2, purl to last 2 sts, k2.

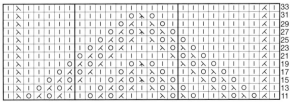

GUSSET CHART

STITCH KEY
- ☐ K on RS, p on WS
- ○ Yo
- ╲ Ssk
- ╱ K2tog
- ⋏ Sk2p

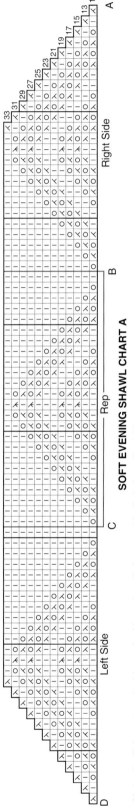

SOFT EVENING SHAWL CHART A

Note: 5 stitches at each side worked in garter stitch are not included on chart. Even number rows not included are worked as: K5, purl to last 5 sts, k5. To work odd-number rows from chart: Work Right Side of shawl from A to C, repeating from B to C as necessary to 3 stitches before marker, then work Gusset Chart. For Left Side of shawl, work from B to C as necessary, working last repeat from B to D

Delicate Lace Shawl

Design by Nazanin Fard

Skill Level

■■■▶ EXPERIENCED

Finished Size

Side to side: approx 87 inches
Top edge to point: approx 37 inches

Materials

- Fiddlesticks Lace Sensation 100% silk lace weight yarn (262 yds/50g per ball): 4 balls lavender
- Size 6 (4.25mm) knitting needles

Gauge

Gauge is not critical for this project.

Special Abbreviations

Slip, slip, knit (ssk): Slip next 2 sts one at a time as if to knit, insert LH needle into fronts of 2 slipped sts and k2tog from this position to dec 1 st.

Slip, slip, purl (ssp): Slip next 2 sts one at a time as if to knit, slip sts back to LH needle keeping them twisted and purl tog through back loops to dec 1 st.

Slip, knit 2 together, pass (sk2p): Slip next st, k2tog, pass slipped st over knit 2 tog and off needle to dec 2 sts.

Pattern Notes

For those preferring to work pattern from a chart Rows 1–9 are shown on Chart A.

Pattern Rows 10–25 are on Chart B. The center knit 1 stitch is not included on chart. Work even-number rows from A to C, knit 1, for center, then work from B to D. Work odd-number rows from D to B, purl 1 for center, then work from C to A.

Rows 26–41 are shown on Chart C. The center knit 1 stitch is not included on chart. Work even-number rows from A to C, knit 1, for center, then work from B to D. Work odd-number rows from D to B, purl 1 for center, then work from C to A.

Rows 42–153 are worked as for Rows 26–41 on Chart C, repeating the marked area an additional time on each repeat of these rows.

Rows 154–159 are worked as given in instructions.

Rows 160–186 are shown on Chart D. The center knit 1 stitch is not included on chart. Work even-number rows from A to C working marked repeat area as necessary, knit 1, for center, then work from B to D working marked repeat area as necessary. Work odd-number rows from D to B, purl 1 for center, then work from C to A.

Odd-number rows not shown on chart are worked as: Knit 2, purl to last 2 sts, knit 2.

Rows 1–8 for Edging are shown on the Edging Chart. The slip, slip, knit at the end of odd-number rows is worked by knitting the last stitch of the

House of White Birches, Berne, Indiana 46711   DRGnetwork.com

edging with the next stitch of the shawl on the needle. Even number rows not included on the chart are knit.

Shawl

Beg at neck edge of center back, cast on 5 sts.

Row 1 (WS): Knit across.

Row 2 (RS): K2, yo, place marker, k1, place marker, yo, k2—7 sts.

Note: Being sure to keep markers on each side of center st, slip markers on following rows as you come to them.

Row 3 and all odd-numbered rows unless otherwise noted: K2, purl to last 2 sts, k2.

Row 4: K2, [yo, k1] 3 times, yo, k2—11 sts.

Row 6: K2, yo, k3, yo, k1, yo, k3, yo, k2—15 sts.

Row 8: K2, yo, k5, yo, k1, yo, k5, yo, k2—19 sts.

Row 10: K2, yo, k3, yo, ssk, k2, yo, k1, yo, k3, yo, ssk, k2, yo, k2.

Row 12: K2, *yo, k2, k2tog, yo, k1, yo, ssk, k2, yo*, k1; rep from * to *, k2.

Row 14: K2, *yo, k2, k2tog, yo, k3, yo, ssk, k2, yo*, k1; rep from * to *, k2.

Row 16: K2, *yo, k3, yo, ssk, yo, sk2p, yo, k2tog, yo, k3, yo*, k1; rep from * to *, k2.

Row 18: K2, *yo, k2, k2tog, yo, k1, yo, ssk, k1, k2tog, yo, k1, yo, ssk, k2, yo*, k1; rep from * to *, k2.

Row 20: K2, *yo, k3, [yo, ssk] twice, k3, [k2tog, yo] twice, k3, yo*, k1; rep from * to *, k2.

Row 21: K2, *p5, [yo, ssp] twice, p1, [p2tog, yo] twice, p5*, p1; rep from * to *, k2.

Row 22: K2, *yo, k6, yo, ssk, yo, sk2p, yo, k2tog, yo, k6, yo*, k1; rep from * to *, k2.

Row 23: K2, *p8, yo, ssp, p1, p2tog, yo, p8*, p1; rep from * to *, k2.

Row 24: K2, *yo, k9, yo, sk2p, yo, k9, yo*, k1; rep from * to *, k2.

Row 25: K2, purl to last 2 sts, k2.

Row 26: K2, *yo, k3, yo, ssk, k14, yo, ssk, k2, yo*, k1; rep from * to *, k2.

Row 28: K2, *yo, k2, k2tog, yo, k1, yo, ssk, k11, k2tog, yo, k1, yo, ssk, k2, yo*, k1; rep from * to * k2.

Row 30: K2, *yo, k2, k2tog, yo, k3, yo, ssk, k9, k2tog, yo, k3, yo, ssk, k2, yo*, k1; rep from * to * k2.

Row 32: K2, *yo, k3, yo, ssk, yo, sk2p, yo, k2tog, yo, k9, yo, ssk, yo, sk2p, yo, k2tog, yo, k3, yo*, k1; rep from * to *, k2.

Row 34: K2, *yo, k2, k2tog, yo, k1, yo, ssk, k1, k2tog, yo, k1, yo, ssk, k5, k2tog, yo, k1, yo, ssk, k1, k2tog, yo, k1, yo, ssk, k2, yo*, k1; rep from * to *, k2.

Row 36: K2, *yo, k3, [yo, ssk] twice, k3, [k2tog, yo] twice, k5, [yo, ssk] twice, k3, [k2tog, yo] twice, k3, yo*, k1; rep from * to *, k2.

Row 37: K2, *p5, [yo, ssp] twice, p1, [p2tog, yo] twice, p7, [yo, ssp] twice, p1, [p2tog, yo] twice, p5*, p1; rep from * to *, k2.

Row 38: K2, *yo, k6, yo, ssk, yo, sk2p, yo, k2tog, yo, k9, yo, ssk, yo, sk2p, yo, k2tog, yo, k6, yo*, k1; rep from * to * k2.

Row 39: K2, *p8, yo, ssp, p1, p2tog, yo, p11, yo, ssp, p1, p2tog, yo, p8*, p1; rep from * to *, k2.

Row 40: K2, *yo, k9, yo, sk2p, yo, k13, yo, sk2p, yo, k9, yo*, k1; rep from * to *, k2.

Place marker after first 2 sts and before last 2 sts when working following row.

Row 41: K2, purl to last 2 sts, k2.

Row 42: K2, *yo, k3, [yo, ssk, k14] to 4 sts before marker, yo, ssk, k2, yo*, k1; rep from * to *, k2.

Row 44: K2, *yo, k2, [k2tog, yo, k1, yo, ssk, k11] to 7 sts before marker, k2tog, yo, k1, yo, ssk, k2, yo*, k1; rep from * to *, k2.

Row 46: K2, *yo, k2, [k2tog, yo, k3, yo, ssk, k9] to 9 sts before marker, k2tog, yo, k3, yo, ssk, k2, yo*, k1; rep from * to *, k2.

Row 48: K2, *yo, k3, [yo, ssk, yo, sk2p, yo, k2tog, yo, k9] to 10 sts before marker, yo, ssk, yo, sk2p, yo, k2tog, yo, k3, yo*, k1; rep from * to *, k2.

Row 50: K2, *yo, k2, [k2tog, yo, k1, yo, ssk, k1, k2tog, yo, k1, yo, ssk, k5] to 13 sts before marker, k2tog, yo, k1, yo, ssk, k1, k2tog, yo, k1, yo, ssk, k2, yo*, k1; rep from * to *, k2.

Row 52: K2, *yo, k3, [{yo, ssk} twice, k3, {k2tog, yo} twice, k5] to 14 sts before marker, [yo, ssk] twice, k3, [k2tog, yo] twice, k3, yo*, k1; rep from * to *, k2.

Row 53: K2, *p5, [{yo, ssp} twice, p1, {p2tog, yo} twice, p7] to 14 sts before marker, [yo, ssp] twice, p1, [p2tog, yo] twice, p5*, p1; rep from * to *, k2.

Row 54: K2, *yo, k6, [yo, ssk, yo, sk2p, yo, k2tog, yo, k9] to 13 sts before marker, yo, ssk, yo, sk2p, yo, k2tog, yo, k6, yo*, k1; rep from * to * k2.

Row 55: K2, *p8, [yo, ssp, p1, p2tog, yo, p11] to 13 sts before marker, yo, ssp, p1, p2tog, yo, p8*, p1; rep from * to *, k2.

Row 56: K2, *yo, k9, [yo, sk2p, yo, k13] to 12 sts before marker, yo, sk2p, yo, k9, yo*, k1; rep from * to *, k2.

Row 57: K2, purl to last 2 sts, k2.

Rows 58–153: Rep [Rows 42–57] 6 times.

Row 154: K2, yo, knit to marker, yo, k1, yo, knit to last 2 sts, yo, k2.

Row 155: K2, purl to last 2 sts, p2.

Rows 156–159: Rep [Rows 154 and 155] twice. At end of Row 159—319 sts.

Row 160: K2, *yo, [k1, yo, ssk, k7, k2tog, yo] to st before marker, k1, yo*, k1 (center st); rep from * to *, k2.

Row 162: K2, *yo, k1, [k2, yo, ssk, k5, k2tog, yo, k1] to 2 sts before marker, k2, yo*, k1; rep from * to *, k2.

Row 164: K2, *yo, k2, [k3, yo, ssk, k3, k2tog, yo, k2] to 3 sts before marker, k3, yo*, k1; rep from * to *, k2.

Row 166: K2, *yo, k3, [k4, yo, ssk, k1, k2tog, yo, k3] to 4 sts before marker, k4, yo*, k1; rep from * to *, k2.

Row 168: K2, *yo, k4, [k5, yo, sk2p, yo, k4] to 5 sts before marker, k5, yo*, k1; rep from * to *, k2.

Row 170: K2, *yo, k3, k2tog, yo, [k1, yo, ssk, k1, k2tog, yo] to 6 sts before marker, k1, yo, ssk, k3, yo*, k1; rep from * to *, k2.

Row 172: K2, *yo, k4, k2tog, yo, [k1, yo, ssk, k1, k2tog, yo] to 7 sts before marker, k1, yo, ssk, k4, yo*, k1; rep from * to *, k2.

Row 174: K2, *yo, k5, k2tog, yo, [k1, yo, ssk, k1, k2tog, yo] to 8 sts before marker, k1, yo, ssk, k5, yo*, k1; rep from * to *, k2.

Row 176: K2, *yo, k6, k2tog, yo, [k1, yo, ssk, k1, k2tog, yo] to 9 sts before marker, k1, yo, ssk, k6, yo*, k1; rep from * to *, k2.

Row 178: K2, *yo, k7, k2tog, yo, [k1, yo, ssk, k7, k2tog, yo] to 10 sts before marker, k1, yo, ssk, k7, yo*, k1; rep from * to *, k2.

Row 180: K2, *yo, k7, k2tog, yo, k1, [k2, yo, ssk, k5, k2tog, yo, k1] to 11 sts before marker, k2, yo, ssk, k7,

yo*, k1; rep from * to *, k2.

Row 182: K2, *yo, k7, k2tog, yo, k2, [k3, yo, ssk, k3, k2tog, yo, k2] to 12 sts before marker, k3, yo, ssk, k7, yo*, k1; rep from * to *, k2.

Row 184: K2, *yo, k7, k2tog, yo, k3, [k4, yo, ssk, k1, k2tog, yo, k3] to 13 sts before marker, k4, yo, ssk, k7, yo*, k1; rep from * to *, k2.

Row 186: K2, *yo, k7, k2tog, yo, k4, [k5, yo, sk2p, yo, k4] to 14 sts before marker, k5, yo, ssk, k7, yo*, k1; rep from * to *, k2.

Row 187: K2, purl to last 2 sts, k2.

Row 188: K2, yo, knit to marker, yo, k1, yo, knit to last 2 sts, yo, k2.

Rows 189–192: Rep [Rows 187 and 188] twice.

Edging
Provisionally cast on 9 sts.

With RS of shawl facing you work the edging as follows:

Row 1 (RS): Sl 1p, k1, yo, k2tog, yo, k4, ssk (the last st of the edging with the next st on the body of the shawl)—10 sts.

Row 2 and all even-numbered rows: Knit across.

Row 3: Sl 1p, k1, [yo, k2tog] twice, yo, k3, ssk (the last st of the edging with the next st on the body of the shawl)—11 sts.

Row 5: Sl 1p, k1, [yo, k2tog] 3 times, yo, k2, ssk (the last st of the edging with the next st on the body of the shawl)—12 sts.

Row 7: Sl 1p, k2tog, [yo, k2tog] 3 times, k2, ssk (the last st of the edging with the next st on the body of the shawl)—11 sts.

Row 9: Sl 1p, k2tog, [yo, k2tog] twice, k3, ssk (the last st of the edging with the next st on the body of the shawl)—10 sts.

Row 11: Sl 1p, k2tog, yo, k2tog, k4, ssk (the last st of the edging with the next st on the body of the shawl)—9 sts.

Row 12: Knit across.

Rep Rows 1–12 until all sts of the body are bound off. ❖

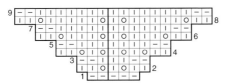

DELICATE LACE SHAWL CHART A

STITCH KEY
- ☐ K on RS, p on WS
- ⊟ P on RS, k on WS
- ⊙ Yo
- ⊼ Ssk on RS, ssp on WS
- ⊠ K2tog on RS, p2tog on WS
- ⋏ Sk2tp

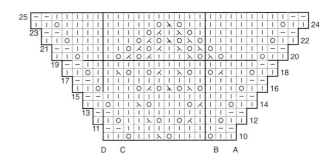

DELICATE LACE SHAWL CHART B

Note: *Center st is not included on chart.*
Work even-number rows from A to C, k1
for center st, then work from B to D.
Work odd-number rows from D to B, p1
for center st, then work from C to A.

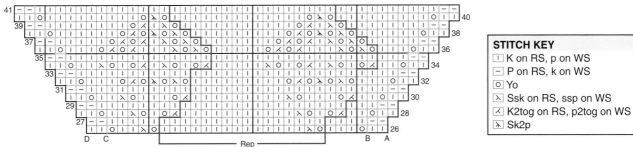

DELICATE LACE SHAWL CHART C

STITCH KEY
- ☐ K on RS, p on WS
- ⊟ P on RS, k on WS
- ⊙ Yo
- ⊼ Ssk on RS, ssp on WS
- ⊠ K2tog on RS, p2tog on WS
- ⋏ Sk2p

Note: *Center st is not included on chart.*
Work even-number rows from A to C, k1 for center st, then work from B to D.
Work odd-number rows from D to B, p1 for center st, then work from C to A.

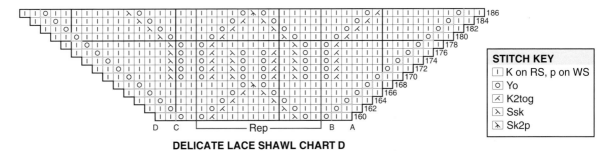

DELICATE LACE SHAWL CHART D

STITCH KEY
- ☐ K on RS, p on WS
- ⊙ Yo
- ⊠ K2tog
- ⊼ Ssk
- ⋏ Sk2p

Note: *WS rows are not included on chart and should be worked as: K2, purl to last 2 sts, k2.*
Center st is not included on chart.
Work even-number rows from A to C working marked repeat area as necessary, k1 for center
st, then work from B to D.
Work odd-number rows from D to B working marked repeat area as necessary, p1 for center st,
then work from C to A.

DELICATE LACE SHAWL EDGING

Note: *WS rows not included on*
chart are knit across.

STITCH KEY
- ☐ K on the RS
- ⊙ Yo
- ⊠ K2tog
- ⊼ Ssk
- • Sl st

Lovely Lace Table Set

Design by Nazanin Fard

Skill Level
 INTERMEDIATE

Finished Sizes
Place mat: 19 inches x 12½ inches
Napkin ring: 1½ inch circumference

Materials
- DMC Baroque 100% mercerized cotton size 10 crochet thread (400 yds per skein): 1 skein white for each place mat and napkin ring set
- Size 1 (2.25mm) knitting needles
- Fabric stiffener
- Cardboard inside roll of toilet paper or paper towel
- Plastic bag
- Blocking board
- Rust-proof T-pins

Gauge
Exact gauge is not critical for this project.

Special Abbreviation
Slip, knit 2 together, pass (sk2p): Slip next st, k2tog, pass slipped st over knit st and off needle to dec 2 sts.

Pattern Notes
Pattern repeat for the center of the place mat, increases on Row 2, original count is restored on Row 4.
Charts included for place mat center and edging for those preferring to work pattern stitches from a chart.

Place Mat

Center
Cast on 91 sts.

Row 1 (WS): Purl across.

Row 2 (RS): P2, *ssk, [yo, k1] 3 times, yo, k2tog, p1; rep from * to last st, p1.

Row 3: K2, purl to last 2 sts, k2.

Row 4: P2, *ssk, k5, k2tog, p1; rep from * to last st, p1.

Row 5: K2, purl to last 2 sts, k2.

Rep [Rows 2–5] 24 times.

Rep Rows 2–4.

Do not bind off.

Edging
Note: When working the edging, the last k2tog of odd numbered rows is made by working 1 st from the edging and 1 st from the body of the place mat. For the 3 sides that have no live stitches, pick up 1 st at the edge and knit it tog with the last st of the edging.

Cable cast on 8 sts.

Row 1 (RS): K7, k2tog (1 st from edging and 1 st from place mat).

Row 2: Sl 1, ssk, cast on 4 sts, k2, k2tog, k1—10 sts.

Row 3: K9, k2tog (1 st from edging and 1 st from place mat).

Row 4: Sl 1, ssk, [yo, k1] 4 times, yo, k2tog, k1—13 sts.

Row 5: K12, k2tog (1 st from edging and 1 st from place mat).

Row 6: Sl 1, ssk, [yo, k1] twice, yo, sk2p, [yo, k1] twice, yo, k2tog, k1—15 sts.

Row 7: K14, k2tog (1 st from edging and 1 st from place mat).

Row 8: Sl 1, k12, k2tog—14 sts.

Row 9: Bind off 6 sts, k7 (including last bind off), k2tog (1 st from edging and 1 st from place mat)—8 sts.

Rep Rows 2–9 for pat.

Bind off loosely.

Napkin Ring
Cast on 11 sts.

Row 1 (WS): K2, p7, k2.

Row 2: P2, ssk, [yo, k1] 3 times, yo, k2tog, p2—13 sts.

Row 2: Sl 1, ssk, cast on 4 sts, k2, k2tog, k1—10 sts.

Row 3: K9, k2tog (1 st from edging and 1 st from napkin ring).

Row 4: Sl 1, ssk, [yo, k1] 4 times, yo, k2tog, k1—13 sts.

Row 5: K12, k2tog (1 st from edging and 1 st from napkin ring).

Row 6: Sl 1, ssk, [yo, k1] twice, yo, sk2p, [yo, k1] twice, yo, k2tog, k1—15 sts.

Row 7: K14, k2tog (1 st from edging and 1 st from napkin ring).

Row 8: Sl 1, k12, k2tog—14 sts.

Row 9: Bind off 6 sts, k7 (includes last bind off), k2tog (1 st from edging and 1 st from napkin ring) —8 sts.

Rep Rows 2–9 for pat.

Bind off loosely.

Row 3: K2, purl to last 2 sts, k2.

Row 4: P2, ssk, k5, k2tog, p2—11 sts.

Row 5: K2, purl to last 2 sts.

Rep Rows 2–5 until piece wraps around the toilet paper roll. Bind off all sts.

Edging

Note: *Edging is worked along length of one edge of napkin ring. The last k2tog of odd numbered rows is made by working 1 st from the edging and picking up 1 st from the edge of the napkin ring together.*

Cast on 8 sts.

Row 1 (RS): Knit first 7 edging sts, with RS of napkin ring facing, k2tog (1 st from edging and 1 st from napkin ring).

Finishing

Sew the side of napkin ring.

Dilute fabric stiffener in water and place the place mat and napkin ring in the solution for 15 minutes. Take them out. Spread the place mat on blocking board and pin it to size and let dry.

Wrap the outside of the toilet paper roll in plastic. Insert it in the napkin ring. Stand it up on the bottom edge and let the napkin ring dry. ❖

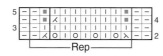

LOVELY LACE TABLE SET PLACE MAT CHART

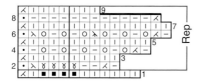

LOVELY LACE TABLE SET EDGING CHART

STITCH KEY
| K on RS, p on WS
— P on RS, k on WS
○ Yo
/ K2tog
\ Ssk
• Sl1
↗ Sk2p
ᵛ Cast on
■ No stitch
— Bind off 6 sts

Pineapple & Diamonds Table Runner

Design by Nazanin Fard

Skill Level

 **INTERMEDIATE**

Finished Size

Approx 22 inches wide x 42 inches long, after blocking

Materials

- Aunt Lydia's Classic Crochet 100% mercerized cotton size 10 crochet thread (1,000 yds per ball): 1 ball white #201
- Size 1 (2.25mm) straight and 29-inch long knitting needles or size needed to obtain gauge
- Size 7 (1.65mm) crochet hook
- 1 dark color and 39 light color ring-type markers
- Rustproof straight pins
- Blocking board
- Fabric stiffener or spray starch

Gauge

16 sts = 2 inches in St st.
To save time, take time to check gauge.

Special Abbreviations

Slip, slip, knit (ssk): Slip next 2 sts one at a time as if to knit, insert LH needle into fronts of 2 slipped sts and k2tog from this position to dec 1 st.

Slip, knit 2 together, pass (sk2p): Slip next st, k2tog, pass slipped st over knit st and off needle to dec 2 sts.

Table Runner

First End

With straight needles, cast on 5 sts.

Rows 1 and 2: Knit across.

Row 3: K2, yo, k1, yo, k2—7 sts.

Row 4 and all even-numbered rows: K2, purl to last 2 sts, k2.

Row 5: K2, yo, k3, yo, k2—9 sts.

Row 7: K2, yo, k5, yo, k2—11 sts.

Row 9: K2, yo, k7, yo, k2—13 sts.

Row 11: K2, yo, k1, *yo, ssk, k3, k2tog, yo, k1; rep from * to last 2 sts, yo, k2—15 sts.

Row 13: K2, yo, k3, yo, ssk, k1, k2tog, yo, k3; rep from * to last 2 sts, yo, k2—17 sts.

Row 15: K2, yo, k5, *yo, sk2p, yo, k5; rep from * to last 2 sts, yo, k2—19 sts.

Row 17: K2, yo, k6, *k2tog, yo, k6; rep from * to last 3 sts, k1, yo, k2—21 sts.

Rows 19–98: Rep [Rows 11–18] 10 times. At end of Row 98—101 sts.

Row 99: For center section: K2, yo, ssk, k4, *k2tog, yo, k1, yo, ssk, k3; rep from * to last 5 sts, k1, k2tog, yo, k2—101 sts.

Row 101: K2, [yo, ssk] twice, k1, *k2tog, yo, k3, yo, ssk, k1; rep from * to last 6 sts, [k2tog, yo] twice, k2.

Row 103: K2, yo, ssk, k1, *yo, sk2p, yo, k5; rep from * to last 8 sts, yo, sk2p, yo, k1, k2tog, yo, k2.

Row 105: K2, yo, ssk, k1, *k2tog, yo, k6; rep from * to last 8 sts, k2tog, yo, k2, k2tog, yo, k2.

Row 107: K2, yo, ssk, *k2tog, yo, k1, yo, ssk, k3; rep from * to last 9 sts, k2tog, yo, k1, yo, ssk, k2tog, yo, k2.

Row 109: K2, yo, sk2p, yo, k3, *yo, ssk, k1, k2tog, yo, k3; rep from * to last 5 sts, yo, sk2p, yo, k2.

Row 111: K2, yo, ssk, k5, *yo, sk2p, yo, k5; rep from * to last 4 sts, k2tog, yo, k2.

Row 113: K2, yo, ssk, k5, *k2tog, yo, k6; rep from * to last 4 sts, k2tog, yo, k2.

Rows 115–306: Rep [Rows 99–114] 12 times—13 half-diamonds along each side of center section.

Row 307: K2, yo, sk2p, *k3, k2tog, yo, k1, yo, ssk; rep from * to last 5 sts, sk2p, yo, k2—99 sts.

Row 309: K2, yo, sk2p, *k1, k2tog, yo, k3, yo, ssk; rep from * to last 8 sts, k3, sk2p, yo, k2—97 sts.

Row 311: K2, yo, sk2p, k1, pass the previous st over the st just made and off needle, yo, k5, *yo, sk2p, yo, k5; rep from * to last 6 sts, sk2p, k1, pass the previous st over the st just made and off needle, yo, k2—95 sts.

Row 313: K2, yo, sk2p, k5, *k2tog, yo, k6; rep from * to last 5 sts, sk2p, yo, k2—93 sts.

Rows 315–386: Rep [Rows 307–314] 9 times—21 sts.

Rows 387–390: Rep Rows 307–310—17 sts.

Row 391: K2, yo, sk2p, k1, pass the previous st over the st just made and off needle, yo, k5, yo, k1, sk2p, pass the previous st over the st just made and off needle, yo, k2—15 sts.

Row 393: K2, yo, sk2p, k5, sk2p, yo, k2—13 sts.

Row 395: K2, yo, sk2p, k3, sk2p, yo, k2—11 sts.

Row 397: K2, yo, sk2p, k1, sk2p, yo, k2—9 sts

Row 399: K2, yo, sk2p, yo, k2—7 sts.

Row 401: K2, sk2p, k2—5 sts.

Do not work even-numbered row.

Bind off purlwise; turn; do not cut thread.

Border

With circular needle, pick up and knit in each of 5 bound-off sts; pick up and knit 195 sts evenly spaced in ends of rows to cast-on edge, pick up and knit in each of 5 cast-on sts, pick up and knit 195 evenly spaced in ends of rows to first st—400 sts. Join.

Rnd 1: Place dark marker for beg of rnd, k2, yo, ssk, k3, k2tog, yo, k1, *place light marker, k2, yo, ssk, k3, k2tog, yo, k1; rep from * around—10 sts in each rep between markers.

Note: Slip markers on following rnds when you come to them.

Rnd 2 and all even-numbered rnds: Knit around.

Rnd 3: *K3, yo, ssk, k1, k2tog, yo, k2; rep from * around.

Rnd 5: *K1, yo, k3, yo, k3tog, yo, k3, yo; rep from * around—12 sts in each rep.

Rnd 7: *(K1, yo, k1, yo, k1) all in next st, yo, ssk, k1, k2tog, yo, k1, yo, ssk, k1, k2tog, yo; rep from * around—16 sts in each rep.

Rnd 9: *K5, yo, ssk, k1, k2tog, yo, k1, yo, ssk, k1, k2tog, yo; rep from * around.

Rnd 11: *[K1, yo] 5 times, ssk, k1, k2tog, yo, k1, yo, ssk, k1, k2tog, yo; rep from * around—20 sts in each rep.

Rnd 13: *K9, yo, ssk, k1, k2tog, yo, k1, yo, ssk, k1, k2tog, yo; rep from * around.

Rnd 15: *[Ssk, yo] twice, k1, [yo, k2tog] twice, yo, ssk, k1, k2tog, yo, (k1, yo, k1, yo, k1) all in next st, yo, ssk, k1, k2tog, yo; rep from * around—24 sts in each rep.

Rnd 17: *Ssk, yo, k1, sk2p, k1, yo, k2tog, yo, ssk, k1, k2tog, yo, k5, yo, ssk, k1, k2tog, yo; rep from * around—22 sts in each rep.

Rnd 19: *Ssk, yo, sk2p, yo, k2tog, yo, ssk, k1, k2tog, yo, [k1, yo] 5 times, ssk, k1, k2tog, yo; rep from * around—24 sts in each rep.

Rnd 21: *Ssk, k1, k2tog, yo, ssk, k1, [k2tog, yo] 3 times, k1, [yo, ssk] 3 times, k1, k2tog, yo; rep from * around—22 sts in each rep.

Rnd 23: *Sk2p, yo, ssk, k1, k2tog, (yo, k1) 9 times, yo, ssk, k1, k2tog, yo; rep from * around—28 sts in each rep.

Rnd 25: *Remove marker, slip end yo on RH needle to LH needle, replace marker on RH needle, sk2p, k2, k2tog, yo, k17, yo, ssk, k2; rep from * around leaving last st unworked—26 sts in each rep.

Rnd 27: *Slip end st on LH needle to RH needle, remove marker, slip end st on RH needle back to LH needle, replace marker on RH needle, sk2p, k1, k2tog, yo, k17, yo, ssk, k1; rep from * around leaving last st unworked—24 sts in each rep.

Rnd 29: *Slip end st on LH needle to RH needle, remove marker, slip end st on RH needle back to LH needle, replace marker on RH needle, sk2p, [k2tog, yo] 5 times, k1, [yo, ssk] 5 times; rep from * around leaving last st unworked—24 sts in each rep.

Rnd 31: *Slip end st on LH needle to RH needle, remove marker, slip end st on RH needle back to LH

continued on page 46

Easy Lace Coasters

Design by Nazanin Fard

Skill Level

 INTERMEDIATE

Finished Size
About 5½ inches square

Materials
- DMC Traditions 100% mercerized cotton size 10 crochet thread (350 yds per ball): 1 ball red #5321
- Size 1 (2.25mm) knitting needles
- Rustproof pins
- Blocking board
- Fabric stiffener
- Tapestry needle

Gauge
26 sts and 40 rows = 4 inches/10cm.
Gauge is not critical for this project.

Pattern Notes
Slip the first stitch of each row of coaster center purlwise to make it easier to pick stitches when working the edging.

Charts are included for those preferring to work pattern for center and edging from a chart. On chart for center odd-numbered rows are worked from right to left on the right side of work and even-numbered rows are worked from left to right on wrong side of work. On chart for edging odd-numbered rows are worked from right to left on wrong side of work and even-numbered rows are worked from left to right on the right side of work.

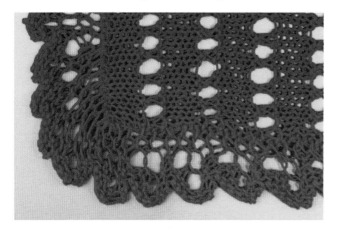

Edging is worked perpendicular to the edge of the coaster. The knit 2 together at the end of odd-numbered rows is worked by knitting the last stitch of the edging with 1 stitch on the center of the coaster, either live or picked up.

When knitting in double yarn overs, knit in the first yarn over and purl into the back of the second yarn over.

Coaster Center
Make 4

Cast on 27 sts.

Row 1 (RS): Sl 1p, knit across.

Row 2: Sl 1p, purl across.

Rows 3 and 4: Rep Rows 1 and 2.

Rows 5 and 6: Rep Row 1.

Row 7: Sl 1p, k1, *yo, k2tog; rep from * to last st, k1.

Row 8: Rep Row 1.

Rows 9–32: Rep [Rows 1–8] 3 times.

Rows 33–37: Rep Rows 1–5.

Do not bind off.

Edging
Cable cast on 5 sts.

Row 1 (WS): K4, k2tog (1 st from edging and 1 st from coaster).

Row 2 (RS): Sl 1p, [k1, wrap yarn twice around needle] twice, k2.

Row 3: K2, (k1, p1) in double yo, k1, (k1, p1) in double yo, k1, k2tog (1 st from edging and 1 st from coaster)—9 sts.

Row 4: Sl 1p, knit across.

Row 5: Bind off 4 sts, k4 (includes loop on needle after bind off), k2tog (1 st from edging and 1 st from coaster).

Row 6: Sl 1p, k1, yo, k2tog, k1.

Rep Rows 1–6 around the edge of the coaster.

Bind off all sts loosely leaving an 8" tail.

Finishing

Sew the beginning and end of the edging. Weave in all ends.

Dilute fabric stiffener in water. Place coasters in the solution for 15 minutes. Pin the edging points while stretching to size. Let dry. ❖

**EASY LACE COASTERS
EDGING CHART**

**EASY LACE COASTERS
CENTER CHART**

STITCH KEY
- ⊡ K on RS, p on WS
- ⊟ P on RS, k on WS
- ⊙ Yo
- ⊠ K2tog
- ⊡ Sl 1p
- — Bind off 4 sts

House of White Birches, Berne, Indiana 46711   DRGnetwork.com

Pineapple Coaster

Design by Nazanin Fard

Skill Level

 INTERMEDIATE

Finished Size

About 6½ square, after blocking

Materials

- Aunt Lydia's Classic Crochet 100% mercerized cotton size 10 crochet thread (1,000 yds per ball): 50 yds white #201 (for each coaster)
- Size 1 (2.75mm) set of 5 double-point needles or size needed to obtain gauge
- Size 7 (1.65mm) steel crochet hook
- Stitch marker
- Rustproof straight pins
- Blocking board
- Fabric stiffener or spray starch

Gauge

16 sts = 2 inches in St st.
To save time, take time to check gauge.

Special Abbreviations

Slip, slip, knit (ssk): Slip next 2 sts one at a time as if to knit, insert LH needle into fronts of 2 slipped sts and k2tog from this position to dec 1 st.

Slip, knit 2 together, pass (sk2p): Slip next st, k2tog, pass slipped st over knit st and off needle to dec 2 sts.

Pattern Note

Coaster is worked in rounds beginning at center on double-point needles. Mark first stitch of round.

Coaster

Cast 12 sts onto 1 double-point needle.

Rnd 1: [With separate needle, k3] 4 times—3 sts on each of 4 needles.

Rnd 2: [K1, yo, k1, yo, k1] on each needle—5 sts on each needle.

Rnds 3 and 4: Knit around.

Rnd 5: *K1, yo; rep from * around—10 sts on each needle.

Rnds 6 and 7: Knit around.

Rnd 8: *K1, yo, k2tog, k5, ssk, yo; rep from * on each needle.

Rnd 9 and all odd-numbered rnds: Knit around.

Rnd 10: *Yo, ssk, k2tog, yo, (k1, yo, k1, yo, k1) in next st, yo, ssk, k2tog, yo, k1; rep from * on each needle—14 sts on each needle.

Rnd 12: *Yo, ssk, k2tog, yo, k5, yo, ssk, k2tog, yo, k1; rep from * on each needle.

Rnd 14: *Yo, ssk, k2tog, yo, [k1, yo] 5 times, ssk, k2tog, yo, k1; rep from * on each needle—18 sts on each needle.

Rnd 16: *Yo, ssk, k2tog, yo, k9, yo, k2tog, ssk, yo, k1; rep from * on each needle.

Rnd 18: *Yo, ssk, k2tog, yo, [ssk, yo] twice, k1, [yo, k2tog] twice, yo, k2tog, ssk, yo, k1; rep from * on each needle.

Rnd 20: *Yo, ssk, k2tog, yo, ssk, yo, k1, sk2p, k1, yo, k2tog, yo, ssk, k2tog, yo, (k1, yo, k1, yo, k1) in next st; rep from * on each needle—20 sts on each needle.

Rnd 22: *Yo, ssk, k2tog, yo, ssk, yo, sk2p, yo, k2tog, yo, ssk, k2tog, yo, k5; rep from * on each needle—18 sts on each needle.

Rnd 24: *Yo, ssk, k2tog, yo, ssk, k1, k2tog, yo, ssk, k2tog, yo, [k1, yo] 4 times, k1; rep from * on each needle—20 sts on each needle.

Rnd 26: *Yo, ssk, k2tog, yo, sk2p, yo, ssk, k2tog, yo, [k1, yo] 8 times, k1; rep from * on each needle—26 sts on each needle.

Rnd 28: *Yo, ssk, k1, sk2p, k1, k2tog, yo, k17; rep from * on each needle—24 sts on each needle.

Rnd 30: *Yo, ssk, sk2p, k2tog, yo, [k1, yo] 16 times, k1; rep from * on each needle—38 sts on each needle.

Set aside fifth (working) needle; with fourth needle, knit the first st on first needle, moving it from beginning of rnd to end of rnd. Remove stitch marker.

Rnd 31: With crochet hook, *[insert crochet hook into each of next 3 sts and remove sts from knitting needle *(see Fig. 1 on page 47),* yo and pull through all loops on hook, Fig. 2 (sc dec made), ch 7] 6 times, *insert crochet hook in each of next 2 sts and remove sts from knitting needle, yo and pull through all loops on hook, ch 7, [insert crochet hook in each of next 3 sts and remove sts from knitting needle, yo and pull through all loops on hook, ch 7] 12 times; rep from * twice more, insert crochet hook in each of next 2 sts and remove sts from knitting needle, yo and pull through all loops on hook, ch 7, [insert crochet hook in each of next 3 sts and remove sts from knitting needle, yo and pull through all loops on hook, ch 7] 6 times, join with sl st in first sc dec. Fasten off.

Finishing

Spread knitted piece on blocking board, stretch to shape, and pin the chain loops in place.

Spray knitted piece lightly with fabric stiffener or starch; let dry, then remove pins. ❖

House of White Birches, Berne, Indiana 46711   DRGnetwork.com

Simple Table Runner

Design by Nazanin Fard

Skill Level

 INTERMEDIATE

Finished Size

Approx 17½ X 35 inches

Materials

- J. & P. Coats Royale Classic Crochet Large Ball 100% mercerized cotton size 10 crochet thread (2,730 yds per ball): 1 ball white #201
- Size 1 (2.25mm) straight and circular needles or size needed to obtain gauge
- Stitch markers
- Rustproof T-pins
- Blocking board
- Fabric stiffener

Gauge

30 sts and 36 rows = 4 inches/10cm in St st.
To save time, take time to check gauge.

Special Abbreviation

Slip 2, knit 1, pass 2 over (sl2kp2sso): Slip next 2 sts, k1, pass 2 slipped sts over knit st and off needle to dec 2 sts.

Pattern Notes

Center of runner is worked on straight needles in Stockinette stitch. Edging is worked in rounds on a circular needle. A chart is provided for the edging beginning with Round 3 for those preferring to work the pattern from a chart. Only the odd-number pattern rounds are shown on the chart. All even-number rounds are knit.

When working the edging, it is helpful to place a different color marker at the beginning of the edging round. Slip all markers as you come to them.

Runner

Center

With straight needles, cast on 101 sts.

Work in St st until piece measures about 33½ inches ending with a WS row.

Edging

Change to circular needle.

Knit across sts on needle, pick up and knit 151 sts on one long side, 101 sts across cast on edge, 151 sts on the other long side—504 sts.

Rnd 1: *K1, yo, k100, yo, place marker, k1, yo, place marker, k150, yo, place marker; rep from * once.

Rnd 2 and all even numbered rows: Knit around.

Rnd 3: *[K1, yo, k1, {yo, ssk} twice, k1, {k2tog, yo} twice] to 2 sts before marker, k1, yo, k1; rep from * around.

Rnd 5: *K1, [k1, yo, k2, yo, ssk, yo, sl2kp2sso, yo, k2tog, yo, k1] to 3 sts before marker, k1, yo, k2; rep from * around.

Rnd 7: *K2, [k1, yo, k1, {yo, ssk} twice, k1, {k2tog, yo} twice] to 4 sts before marker, k1, yo, k3; rep from * around.

Rnd 9: *K3, [k1, yo, k2, yo, ssk, yo, sl2kp2sso, yo, k2tog, yo, k1] to 5 sts before marker, k1, yo, k4; rep from * around.

Rnd 11: *K4, *[k1, yo, k1, {yo, ssk} twice, k1, {k2tog, yo} twice] to 6 sts left before marker, k1, yo, k5; rep from * around.

Rnd 13: *K5, [k1, yo, k2, yo, ssk, yo, sl2kp2sso, yo, k2tog, yo, k1] to 7 sts before marker, k1, yo, k6; rep from * around.

Rnds 15 and 17: Purl.

Bind off all sts loosely.

Finishing

Dilute stiffener in water. Soak the runner in the solution for 15 minutes. Spread on the blocking board and pin the tips pulling them out as shown in photo. Let dry. ❖

SIMPLE TABLE RUNNER EDGING CHART

STITCH KEY
- K on RS, p on WS
- P on RS, k on WS
- Yo
- K2tog
- Ssk
- Sl2kp2sso

Lacy Bread Basket Cover

Design by Nazanin Fard

Skill Level

 INTERMEDIATE

Finished Size

Approx 16 inches square

Materials

- DMC Traditions 100% mercerized cotton size 10 crochet thread (400 yds per ball): 1 ball bright white
- Size 1 (2.25mm) straight and 40-inch circular knitting needles
- Size 7 (1.65mm) steel crochet hook
- Stitch marker
- Rustproof pins
- Blocking board

Gauge

Gauge is not critical for this project.

Special Abbreviation

Slip, knit 2 together, pass (sk2p): Slip next st, k2tog, pass slipped st over k2tog and off needle to dec 2 sts.

Pattern Notes

Slip the first stitch of each row purlwise to make it easier to pick up stitches when working on the edging.

Charts for center pattern and edging are included for those preferring to work pattern stitches from a chart. Only right side rows are included on center

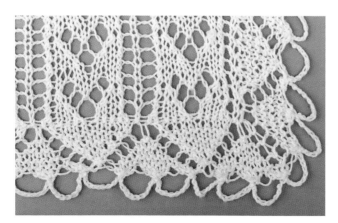

chart. Wrong side rows are worked as: Slip 1 purlwise, purl across.

Center

Cast on 87 sts.

Row 1 and all odd numbered rows (WS): Sl 1p, purl across.

Row 2: Sl 1p, *k1, yo, ssk, k3, yo, ssk, k2, k2tog, yo; rep from * across to last 2 sts, k2.

Row 4: Sl 1p, *k1, yo, ssk, k1, k2tog, yo, k1, yo, ssk, k1, k2tog, yo; rep from * across to last 2 sts, k2.

Row 6: Sl 1p, *k1, yo, ssk, k2tog, yo, k3, yo, ssk, k2tog, yo; rep from * to last 2 sts, k2.

Row 8: Sl 1p, *k1, yo, ssk, k7, k2tog, yo; rep from * across to last 2 sts, k2.

Rep [Rows 1–8] 13 times. Do not bind off.

Edging

Rnd 1: Knit across inc 1 st in last st, place marker, pick up and knit 88 sts on each rem side placing markers at each corner—352 sts.

Rnd 2: *Yo, [k1, yo, ssk, k5, k2tog, yo] to 2 sts before marker, k1, yo, k1; rep from * around—360 sts.

Rnd 3 and all odd-numbered rnds: Purl around.

Rnd 4: *Yo, k1, [k2, yo, ssk, k3, k2tog, yo, k1] to 3 sts before marker, k2, yo, k1; rep from around—368 sts.

Rnd 6: *Yo, k2, [k3, yo, ssk, k1, k2tog, yo, k2] to 4 sts before marker, k3, yo, k1; rep from * around—376 sts.

Rnd 8: *Yo, k3, [k4, yo, sk2p, yo, k3] to 5 sts before marker, k4, yo, k1; rep from * around—384 sts.

Rnd 10: *Insert crochet hook into each of next 4 sts and remove sts from knitting needle (see Fig. 1 on page 47), yo and pull through all loops on hook, Fig. 2 (sc dec made), ch 9; rep from * around, join with slip stitch in first sc dec. Fasten off.

Finishing

Spread out piece on blocking board and pin tight to size. Let dry. ❖

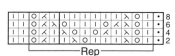

LACY BREAD BASKET COVER CENTER CHART
WS rows not shown on chart are worked
as follows: Sl 1p, purl across.

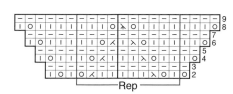

LACY BREAD BASKET COVER EDGING CHART

STITCH KEY

⊐	K on RS, p on WS
−	P on RS, k on WS
O	Yo
⊼	K2tog
⊼	Ssk
•	Sl 1p
⋏	Sk2p

Lacy Bookmark Trio

Design by Nazanin Fard

Triangular Bookmark

Skill Level

 **INTERMEDIATE**

Finished Size
Short sides: 3½ inches
Long side: 5 inches

Materials
- DMC Traditions 100% mercerized cotton size 10 crochet thread (350 yds per ball): 1 ball light green #5369
- Size 0 (2mm) knitting needles or size needed to obtain gauge
- Small ribbon rose for decoration
- Fabric stiffener
- Tapestry needle
- Sewing needle and matching thread

Gauge
28 sts and 30 rows = 4 inches/10cm.
Gauge is not critical for this project.

Special Abbreviation
Slip, slip, knit (ssk): Slip next 2 sts one at a time as if to knit, insert LH needle info fronts of 2 slipped sts and k2tog from this position to dec 1 st.

Pattern Note
Chart is included on page 37 for those preferring to work pattern from a chart.

Bookmark
Make 2

Cast on 5 sts.

Row 1 (RS): Knit across.

Row 2 and all even-numbered rows: K2, purl to last 2 sts, k2.

Row 3: K2, yo, k1, yo, k2—7 sts.

Row 5: K2, yo, k3, yo, k2—9 sts.

Row 7: K2, yo, k5, yo, k2—11 sts.

Row 9: K2, yo, k7, yo, k2—13 sts.

Row 11: K2, yo, k2, k2tog, yo, k1, yo, ssk, k2, yo, k2—15 sts.

Row 13: K2, yo, k2, k2tog, yo, k3, yo, ssk, k2, yo, k2—17 sts.

Row 15: K2, yo, k2, k2tog, yo, k5, yo, ssk, k2, yo, k2—19 sts.

Row 17: K2, yo, k2, k2tog, yo, k7, yo, ssk, k2, yo, k2—21 sts.

Row 19: K2, yo, [k2, k2tog, yo] twice, k1, [yo, ssk, k2] twice, yo, k2—23 sts.

Row 21: K2, yo, [k2, k2tog, yo] twice, k3, [yo, ssk, k2] twice, yo, k2—25 sts.

Row 23: K2, yo, [k2, k2tog, yo] twice, k5, [yo, ssk, k2] twice, yo, k2—27 sts.

Row 25: K2, yo, [k2, k2tog, yo] twice, k7, [yo, ssk, k2] twice, yo, k2—29 sts.

Row 27: K2, yo, [k2, k2tog, yo] twice, [k2tog, yo] twice, k1, [yo, ssk] twice, [yo, ssk, k2] twice, yo, k2—31 sts.

Row 29: K2, yo, k2, k2tog, yo, k19, yo, ssk, k2, yo, k2—33 sts.

Row 31: K2, yo, k2, [k2tog, yo] 6 times, k1, [yo, ssk] 6 times, k2, yo, k2—35 sts.

Rows 33–36: Knit across.

Bind off all sts loosely.

Finishing
Place 2 pieces with WS tog. Sew both short sides. Turn RS out. Dilute fabric stiffener in water and place the bookmark in the solution. Let stand for 15 minutes. Let dry. Referring to photo for placement, sew the ribbon rose on the top corner of the triangle.

Arrowhead Bookmark

Skill Level

■■■□ INTERMEDIATE

Finished Size

10 x 1½ inches, excluding tassel

Materials

- Aunt Lydia's Classic Crochet 100% mercerized cotton size 10 crochet thread (350 yds per ball): 20 yds dusty rose #475
- Size 0 (2mm) knitting needles or size needed to obtain gauge
- Fabric stiffener
- 3-inch-wide piece cardboard (for tassel)

Gauge

28 sts and 30 rows = 4 inches/10cm. Gauge is not critical for this project.

Special Abbreviation

Slip, knit 2 together, pass (sk2p): Slip next st, k2tog, pass slipped st over knit st and off needle to dec 1 st.

Pattern Note

Chart is included for those preferring to work pattern from a chart.

Bookmark

Cast on 13 sts.

Rows 1–4: Knit.

Row 5 (RS): K2, yo, k3, sk2p, k3, yo, k2.

Row 6 and all even-numbered rows: K2, p9, k2.

Row 7: K3, yo, k2, sk2p, k2, yo, k3.

Row 9: K4, yo, k1, sk2p, k1, yo, k4.

Row 11: K5, yo, sk2p, yo, k5.

Row 12: K2, p9, k2.

Rep [Rows 5-12] 11 times.

Knit 4 rows.

Bind off all sts loosely.

Finishing

Weave in all ends.

Dilute fabric stiffener in water. Place the bookmark in the solution for 15 minutes. Spread out and let dry. Make a 3-inch tassel following instructions below:

Tassel

Wrap thread around the cardboard twenty times. Tie a piece of thread about 6 inches long through the loop formed on top of the cardboard holding every piece of thread. Leave the ends for joining to the bookmark. Cut the bottom edge of thread and remove the cardboard.

Wrap another piece of thread around all the strands about ½ inch from the top. Tie securely and cut end as long as the strands in the tassel. Trim the ends. Attach tassel to the pointed edge of the bookmark.

Easy Knitted Bookmark

Skill Level

■■□□ EASY

Finished Size

9½ x 1¼ inches

Materials

- DMC Baroque 100% mercerized cotton, size 10 crochet thread (400 yds per skein): 20 yds ecru
- Size 0 (2mm) knitting needles or size needed to obtain gauge
- One heart-shape button
- Fabric stiffener
- Sewing needle and matching thread

Gauge

28 sts and 30 rows = 4 inches/10cm. Gauge is not critical for this project.

Special Abbreviation

Slip, slip, knit (ssk): Slip next 2 sts one at a time as if to knit, insert LH needle into fronts of 2 slipped sts and k2tog from this position to dec 1 st.

Pattern Note
Chart is included for those preferring to work pattern from a chart.

Bookmark
Cast on 11 sts.

Rows 1–4: Knit across.

Row 5 (RS): K2, yo, ssk, k7.

Row 6 and all even-numbered rows: K2, p7, k2.

Row 7: K3, yo, ssk, k6.

Row 9: K4, yo, ssk, k5.

Row 11: K5, yo, ssk, k4.

Row 13: K6, yo, ssk, k3.

Row 15: K7, yo, ssk, k2.

Row 16: K2, p7, k2.

Rep [Rows 5–16] 9 times.

Rep Rows 1–4.

Finishing
Weave in all ends. Dilute fabric stiffener in water.

Bind off all sts loosely. Place the bookmark in the solution for 15 minutes. Spread out and let dry. Sew button on one end when dry. ❖

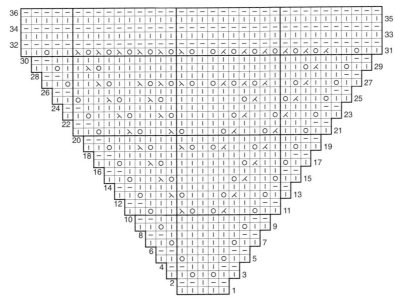

TRIANGULAR BOOKMARK CHART

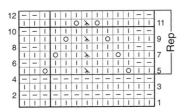

ARROWHEAD BOOKMARK CHART

STITCH KEY
- ⊡ K on RS, p on WS
- ⊟ P on RS, k on WS
- ⊙ Yo
- ⋌ K2tog
- ⋋ Ssk
- ⋊ Sk2p

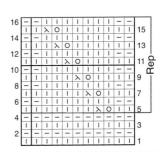

EASY KNITTED BOOKMARK CHART

Lace Star Candle Mat

Design by Nazanin Fard

Skill Level

 INTERMEDIATE

Finished Size

Approx 14 inches across, after blocking.

Materials

- DMC Traditions 100% mercerized cotton size 10 crochet thread (400 yds per ball): 2 balls ecru
- Size 1 (2.25mm) set of 5 double-point needles and 16-inch circular needle or size needed to obtain gauge
- Size 7 (1.65mm) steel crochet hook
- Stitch marker
- Rustproof straight pins or T-pins
- Spray starch or fabric stiffener
- Blocking board

Gauge

15 sts = 2 inches in pat.
To save time, take time to check gauge.

Special Abbreviations

Slip, slip, knit (ssk): Slip next 2 sts one at a time as if to knit, insert LH needle into fronts of 2 slipped sts and k2tog from this position to dec 1 st.

Slip, knit 2 together, pass (sk2p): Slip next st, k2tog, pass slipped st over k2tog and off needle to dec 2 sts.

Pattern Notes

Candle mat is work in rounds starting at the center with double-point needles and changing to a circular needle as necessary to accommodate increased number of stitches.

Place a marker at the beginning of the round. Slip marker when you come to it on following rounds.

Candle Mat

Cast 3 sts onto each of 4 needles; use fifth needle for working—12 sts.

Rnd 1: Knit around.

Rnd 2: *Yo, k1; rep from * around—24 sts.

Rnds 3 and 4: Knit around.

Rnd 5: *Yo, k1; rep from * around—48 sts.

Rnds 6–8: Knit around.

Rnd 9: *Yo, k1; rep from * around—96 sts.

Rnds 10–14: Knit around.

Rnd 15: *Yo, k12; rep from around—104 sts.

Rnd 16 and all even-numbered rnds: Knit around.

Rnd 17: *K1, yo, ssk, k8, k2tog, yo; rep from * around.

Rnd 19: *[K1, yo] twice, ssk, k6, k2tog, yo, k1, yo; rep from * around—120 sts.

Rnd 21: *[K1, yo] 4 times, ssk, k4, k2tog, yo, [k1, yo] 3 times; rep from * around—168 sts.

Rnd 23: *K4, [yo, ssk] 3 times, k2, [k2tog, yo] 3 times, k3; rep from * around.

Rnd 25: *K1, yo, k4, [yo, ssk] 3 times, [k2tog, yo] 3 times, k4, yo; rep from * around—184 sts.

Rnd 27: *[K1, yo] twice, k3, [ssk, yo] 3 times, [k2tog, yo] 3 times, k2tog, k3, yo, k1, yo; rep from * around—208 sts.

Rnd 29: *K1, yo, ssk, yo, k1, yo, k5, [yo, ssk] twice, yo, k1, yo, [k2tog, yo] twice, k5, yo, k1, yo, k2tog, yo; rep from * around—256 sts

Rnd 31: *K2, [yo, ssk] twice, yo, k6, [yo, ssk] twice, k1, [k2tog, yo] twice, k6, yo, [k2tog, yo] twice, k1; rep from * around—272 sts.

Rnd 33: *K1, [yo, ssk] 4 times, k5, yo, ssk, yo, sk2p, yo, k2tog, yo, k5, [k2tog, yo] 4 times; rep from * around.

Rnd 35: *K2, [yo, ssk] 4 times, k5, yo, ssk, k1, k2tog, yo, k5, [k2tog, yo] 4 times, k1; rep from * around.

Rnd 37: *K1, [yo, ssk] 5 times, k5, yo, sk2p, yo, k5, [k2tog, yo] 5 times; rep from * around.

Rnd 39: *K2, [yo, ssk] 5 times, k4, sk2p, k4, [k2tog, yo] 5 times, k1; rep from * around—256 sts.

Rnd 41: *K1, [yo, ssk] 6 times, k7, [k2tog, yo] 6 times; rep from * around.

Rnd 43: *K2, [yo, ssk] 6 times, k5, [k2tog, yo] 6 times, k1; rep from * around.

Rnd 45: *K1, [yo, ssk] 7 times, k3, [k2tog, yo] 7 times; rep from * around.

Rnd 47: *K2, [yo, ssk] 7 times, k1, [k2tog, yo) 7 times, k1; rep from * around.

Rnd 49: *K1, [yo, ssk] 7 times, yo, sk2p, yo, [k2tog, yo) 7 times; rep from * around.

Rnds 50–52: Knit around.

Rnd 53: *Insert crochet hook into each of next 4 sts and remove sts from knitting needle *(see Fig. 1 on page 47)*, yo and pull through all loops on hook, Fig. 2 (sc dec made), ch 9; rep from * around, join in first sc dec. Fasten off.

Finishing

Spray Candle Mat lightly with starch or fabric stiffener.

Spread Candle Mat on blocking board, stretch to shape and pin the chain loops in place until dry. ❖

Pineapple Lap Throw

Design by Nazanin Fard

Skill Level

⬛⬛⬛⬜ INTERMEDIATE

Finished Size

Approx 40 inches square, excluding fringe

Materials

- Red Heart LusterSheen 100% acrylic sport weight yarn (335 yds/113g per skein): 5 skeins white #0001
- Size 5 (3.75mm) set of 5 double-point needles, 16-inch and 29-inch circular needles or size needed to obtain gauge
- Size E/4 (3.5mm) crochet hook
- 1 dark color and 3 light color ring-type markers

Gauge

16 sts = 4 inches/10cm in St st.
To save time, take time to check gauge.

Special Abbreviations

Slip, slip, knit (ssk): Slip next 2 sts one at a time as if to knit, insert LH needle into fronts of 2 slipped sts and k2 tog from this position to dec 1 st.

Slip, knit 2 together, pass (sk2p): Slip next st, k2 tog, pass slipped st over knit st and off needle to dec 2 sts.

Pattern Notes

Throw is worked in rounds from center to outer edge starting with double-point needles and changing to circular needles as stitches are increased.

Mark first stitch of round with dark color marker.

Throw

Cast 8 sts onto one double-point needle.

Rnd 1: [On separate needle, k2] 4 times—2 sts on each of 4 needles; use fifth needle for working.

Join taking care not to twist sts.

Rnd 2: *Yo, k1; rep from * around—4 on each needle.

Rnds 3–5: Knit around.

Rnd 6: *Yo, k1; rep from around—8 sts on each needle.

Rnd 7 and all odd-numbered rnds unless otherwise indicated: Knit around.

Rnd 8: *Yo, k8; rep from * around—9 sts on each needle.

Rnd 10: *K1, yo, knit to last st on same needle, yo, k1; rep from * around—11 sts on each needle.

Rnd 12: Rep Rnd 10—13 sts on each needle.

Rnd 14: *K1, yo, k5, yo, ssk, k4, yo, k1; rep from * around—15 sts on each needle.

Rnd 16: *K1, yo, k4, k2tog, yo, k1, yo, ssk, k4, yo, k1; rep from * around—17 sts on each needle.

Rnd 18: *K1, yo, k4, k2tog, yo, k3, yo, ssk, k4, yo, k1; rep from * around—19 sts on each needle.

Rnd 20: *K1, yo, k2, yo, ssk, k9, k2tog, yo, k2, yo, k1; rep from * around—21 sts on each needle.

Rnd 22: *K1, yo, k3, yo, ssk, k4, yo, ssk, k3, k2tog, yo, k3, yo, k1; rep from * around—23 sts on each needle.

Rnd 24: *K1, yo, k4, yo, ssk, k2, k2tog, yo, k1, yo, ssk, k2, k2tog, yo, k4, yo, k1; rep from * around—25 sts on each needle.

Rnd 26: *K1, yo, k5, yo, ssk, k1, k2tog, yo, k3, yo, ssk, k1, k2tog, yo, k5, yo, k1; rep from * around—27 sts on each needle.

Note: Change to 16-inch circular needle on next rnd. Change to 29-inch circular needle as necessary to accommodate larger number of sts.

Rnd 28: Place dark marker on needle for beg of rnd, k1, yo, k6, yo, ssk, k9, k2tog, yo, k6, yo, k1; *place light marker on needle, k1, yo, k6, yo, ssk, k9, k2tog, yo, k6, yo, k1; rep from * twice—29 sts between markers.

Rnd 30: *K1, yo, k7, yo, ssk, k4, yo, ssk, k3, k2tog, yo, k7, yo, k1; rep from * around slipping markers as you come to them—31 sts between markers.

Rnd 32: *K1, yo, k8, yo, ssk, k2, k2tog, yo, k1, yo, ssk,

k2, k2tog, yo, k8, yo, k1; rep from * around—33 sts between markers.

Rnd 34: *K1, yo, k9, yo, ssk, k1, k2tog, yo, k3, yo, ssk, k1, k2tog, yo, k9, yo, k1; rep from * around—35 sts between markers.

Rnd 35: Knit around.

Rnd 36: *K1, yo, knit to 1 st before next marker, yo, k1; rep from * around—37 sts between markers.

Rnds 37–44: Rep [Rnds 35 and 36] 4 times—45 sts between markers at end of Rnd 44.

Rnd 45: Knit around.

Rnd 46: *K1, yo, k4, k2tog, yo, k1, yo, ssk, [k5, k2tog, yo, k1, yo, ssk] to 5 sts before next marker, k4, yo, k1; rep from * around—47 sts between markers.

Rnd 48: *K1, yo, k4, [k2tog, yo, k3, yo, ssk, k3] to 2 sts before next marker, k1, yo, k1; rep from * around—49 sts between markers.

Rnd 50: *K1, yo, k4, [k2tog, yo, k5, yo, ssk, k1] to 4 sts before next marker, k3, yo, k1; rep from * around—51 sts between markers.

Rnd 52: *K1, yo, k5, **yo, ssk, k2tog, yo, (k1, yo, k1, yo, k1) in next st, yo, ssk, k2tog, yo, k1** rep from ** to ** to 5 sts before next marker, k4, yo, k1; rep from * around—69 sts between markers.

Rnd 54: *K1, yo, k6, [yo, ssk, k2tog, yo, k5, yo, ssk, k2tog, yo, k1] to 6 sts before next marker, k5, yo, k1; rep from * around—71 sts between markers.

Rnd 56: *K1, yo, k7, [yo, ssk, k2tog, yo, {k1, yo}

5 times, ssk, k2tog, yo, k1] to 7 sts before next marker, k6, yo, k1; rep from * around—89 sts between markers.

Rnd 58: *K1, yo, k8, [yo, ssk, k2tog, yo, k9, yo, ssk, k2tog, yo, k1] to 8 sts before next marker, k7, yo, k1; rep from * around—91 sts between markers.

Rnd 60: *K1, yo, k9, **yo, ssk, k2tog, yo, [ssk, yo] twice, k1, [yo, k2tog] twice, yo, ssk, k2tog, yo, k1**; rep from ** to ** to 9 sts before next marker, k8, yo, k1; rep from * around—93 sts between markers.

Rnd 62: *K1, yo, k5, yo, ssk, k2tog, yo, (k1, yo, k1, yo, k1) in next st, yo, ssk, k2tog, yo, **ssk, yo, k1, sk2p, k1, yo, k2tog, yo, ssk, k2tog, yo, (k1, yo, k1, yo, k1) in next st, yo, ssk, k2tog, yo**; rep from ** to ** to 6 sts before next marker, k5, yo, k1; rep from * around—107 sts between markers.

Rnd 64: *K1, yo, k6, yo, ssk, k2tog, yo, k5, yo, ssk, k2tog, yo, [ssk, yo, sk2p, yo, k2tog, yo, ssk, k2tog, yo, k5, yo, ssk, k2tog, yo] to 7 sts before next marker, k6, yo, k1; rep from * around—101 sts between markers.

Rnd 66: *K1, yo, k7, yo, ssk, k2tog, yo, [k1, yo] 5 times, ssk, k2tog, yo, **ssk, k1, k2tog, yo, ssk, k2tog, yo, [k1, yo] 5 times, ssk, k2tog, yo**; rep from ** to ** to 8 sts before next marker, k7, yo, k1; rep from * around—115 sts between markers.

Rnd 68: *K1, yo, k8, yo, ssk, k2tog, yo, k9, yo, ssk, k2tog, yo, [sk2p, yo, ssk, k2tog, yo, k9, yo, ssk, k2tog, yo] to 9 sts before next marker, k8, yo, k1; rep from * around—109 sts between markers.

Rnd 70: *K1, yo, k9, **yo, ssk, k2tog, yo, [ssk, yo] twice, k1, [k2tog, yo] twice, yo, ssk, k2tog, yo, k1**; rep from ** to ** to 9 sts before next marker, k8, yo, k1; rep from * around—111 sts between markers.

Rnd 72: *K1, yo, k10, [yo, ssk, k2tog, yo, ssk, yo, k1, sk2p, k1, yo, k2tog, yo, ssk, k2tog, yo, k1] to 10 sts before next marker, k9, yo, k1; rep from * around—103 sts between markers.

Rnd 74: *K1, yo, k11, [yo, ssk, k2tog, yo, ssk, yo, sk2p, yo, k2tog, yo, ssk, k2tog, yo, k1] to 11 sts before next marker, k10, yo, k1; rep from * around—95 sts between markers.

Rnd 76: *K1, yo, k12, [yo, ssk, k2tog, yo, ssk, k1, k2tog, yo, ssk, k2tog, yo, k1] to 12 sts before next marker, k11, yo, k1; rep from * around—87 sts between markers.

Rnd 78: *K1, yo, k13, yo, ssk, k2tog, yo, sk2p, **yo, ssk, k2tog, yo, k1, yo, ssk, k2tog, yo, sk2p**; rep from ** to ** to 18 sts before next marker, yo, ssk, k2tog, yo, k13, yo, k1; rep from * around—79 sts between markers.

Rnd 79: Knit around.

Rnd 80: *K1, yo, knit to 1 st before next marker, yo, k1; rep from * around.

Rnds 81–88: Rep [Rnds 79 and 80] 3 times—89 sts between markers.

Rnd 89: Rep Rnd 79.

Rnd 90: *K1, yo, k6, k2tog, yo, k1, yo, ssk, [k4, yo, ssk, k3, k2tog, yo, k1, yo, ssk] to 7 sts before next marker, k6, yo, k1; rep from * around—91 sts between markers.

Rnd 92: *K1, yo, k7, [k2tog, yo, k1, yo, ssk, k2] to 6 sts before next marker, k5, yo, k1; rep from * around—93 sts between markers.

Rnd 94: *K1, yo, k8, [k2tog, yo, k1, yo, ssk, k1, k2tog, yo, k3, yo, ssk, k1] to 15 sts before next marker, k2tog, yo, k1, yo, ssk, k8, yo, k1; rep from * around—95 sts between markers.

Rnd 96: *K1, yo, k9, [k2tog, yo, k1, yo, ssk, k9] to 1 st before next marker, yo, k1; rep from * around—97 sts between markers.

Rnd 98: *K1, yo, k10, k2tog, yo, k1, yo, ssk, [k4, yo, ssk, k3, k2tog, yo, k1, yo, ssk] to 11 sts before next marker, k10, yo, k1; rep from * around—99 sts between markers.

Rnd 100: *K1, yo, k11, [k2tog, yo, k1, yo, ssk, k2] to 10 sts before next marker, k9, yo, k1; rep from * around—101 sts between markers.

Rnd 102: *K1, yo, k12, k2tog, yo, k1, yo, ssk, [k1, k2tog, yo, k3, yo, ssk, k1, k2tog, yo, k1, yo, ssk] to 13 sts before next marker, k12, yo, k1; rep from * around—103 sts between markers.

Rnd 104: *K1, yo, k13, [k2tog, yo, k1, yo, ssk, k9] to 5 sts before next marker, k4, yo, k1; rep from * around—105 sts between markers.

Rnd 106: *K1, yo, k2tog, yo, k1, yo, ssk, [k4, yo, ssk, k3, k2tog, yo, k1, yo, ssk] to 1 st before next marker, yo, k1; rep from * around—107 sts between markers.

Rnd 108: *K1, yo, k1, k2tog, yo, k1, yo, ssk, [k2, k2tog, yo, k1, yo, ssk] to 2 sts before next marker, k1, yo, k1; rep from * around—109 sts between markers.

Rnd 110: *K1, yo, k2, k2tog, yo, k1, yo, ssk, [k1, k2tog, yo, k3, yo, ssk, k1, k2tog, yo, k1, yo, ssk] to 3 sts before next marker, k2, yo, k1; rep from * around—111 sts between markers.

Rnd 112: *K1, yo, k3, k2tog, yo, k1, yo, ssk, [k9, k2tog, yo, k1, yo, ssk] to 4 sts before next marker, k3, yo, k1; rep from * around—113 sts between markers.

Rnd 113: Knit around.

Rnd 114: *K1, yo, knit to 1 st before next marker, yo, k1; rep from * around.

Rnds 115–124: Rep [Rnds 79 and 80] 5 times—125 sts between markers.

Rnd 125: Rep Rnd 113.

Rnds 126–158: Rep Rnds 46–78.

Last rnd: *Insert crochet hook into each of next 3 sts and remove sts from knitting needle (*see Fig. 1 on page 47*), yo and pull through all loops on hook, Fig. 2 (sc dec made), ch 9; rep from * around, join with sl st in first sc dec.

Fasten off.

Fringe

For each knot, cut 2 strands each 14 inches long. Holding both strands together as one, fold in half; with crochet hook, from back, pull fold through ch-9 loop, pull ends through fold, pull tight.

Work fringe knots as above in each ch-9 loop around. Trim ends even. ❖

Beaded Lace Lampshade

Design by Nazanin Fard

Skill Level

 INTERMEDIATE

Finished Size
Fits lampshade about 5½ inches across the top x 13 inches across bottom x 8¾ inches high

Materials
- Aunt Lydia's Classic Crochet 100% mercerized cotton size 10 crochet thread (1,000 yds per ball): 1 ball white #201
- Size 1 (2.25mm) 16-inch and 24-inch needle or size needed to obtain gauge
- Size 3 (3.25mm) 24-inch needle or size needed to obtain gauge
- Size 5 (3.75mm) 24-inch needle or size needed to obtain gauge
- Size 7 (1.65mm) steel crochet hook
- Desired lamp shade about 5½ inches across top x 13 inches across bottom x 8¾ inches high
- 1 dark color and 16 light color ring-type stitch markers
- ⅔ yd ½ inch-wide braided trim for top
- 1¼ yds beaded fringe for bottom
- Fabric glue
- Rustproof straight pins
- Tapestry needle

Gauge
16 sts = 2 inches in St st on Size 1 needles.
13 sts = 2 inches in St st on Size 3 needles.
10 sts = 2 inches in St st on Size 5 needles.

Special Abbreviations
Slip, slip, knit (ssk): Slip next 2 sts one at a time as if to knit, insert LH needle into fronts of 2 slipped sts and k2tog from this position to dec 1 st.

Slip, knit 2 together, pass (sk2p): Slip next st, k2tog, pass slipped st over knit st and off needle to dec 2 sts.

Pattern Notes
Cover for lampshade is worked in rounds from top of the shade to the bottom on circular needles. Change needle sizes as indicated.

Slip markers as you come to them.

Lampshade Cover
With shorter length size 1 needle, cast on 170. Being careful not to twist work, join placing dark marker on needle for beg of rnd.

Rnd 1: Knit around.

Rnd 2: Purl around.

Rnds 3 and 4: Knit around.

Rnd 5: K2tog, yo, k1, yo, ssk, k5, *place light marker on needle, k2tog, yo, k1, yo, ssk, k5; rep from * around—10 sts in each rep between markers.

Rnd 6 and all even-numbered rnds: Knit around.

Rnd 7: *K2tog, yo, k3, yo, ssk, k3; rep from * around.

Rnd 9: *K2tog, yo, k5, yo, ssk, k1; rep from * around.

Rnd 11: *Yo, ssk, k2tog, yo, (k1, yo, k1, yo, k1) all in next st, yo, ssk, k2tog, yo, k1; rep from * around—14 sts in each rep between markers.

Rnd 13: *Yo, ssk, k2tog, yo, k5, yo, ssk, k2tog, yo, k1; rep from * around.

Note: Change to 24-inch size 1 needle when sts become too crowded on 16-inch needle.

Rnd 15: *Yo, ssk, k2tog, yo, [k1, yo] 5 times, ssk, k2tog, yo, k1; rep from * around—18 sts in each rep between markers.

Rnd 17: *Yo, ssk, k2tog, yo, k9, yo, ssk, k2tog, yo, k1; rep from * around.

Rnd 19: *Yo, ssk, k2tog, yo, [ssk, yo] twice, k1, [yo, k2tog] twice, yo, ssk, k2tog, yo, k1; rep from * around.

Rnd 21: *Yo, ssk, k2tog, yo, ssk, yo, k1, sk2p, k1, yo, k2tog, yo, ssk, k2tog, yo, (k1, yo, k1, yo, k1) all in next st; rep from *around—20 sts in each rep between markers.

Rnd 23: *Yo, ssk, k2tog, yo, ssk, yo, sk2p, yo, k2tog, yo, ssk, k2tog, yo, k5; rep from * around—18 sts in each rep between markers.

Rnd 25: *Yo, ssk, k2tog, yo, ssk, k1, k2tog, yo, ssk, k2tog, [yo, k1] 5 times; rep from * around—20 sts in each rep between markers.

Rnd 27: *Yo, ssk, k2tog, yo, sk2p, yo, ssk, k2tog, yo, k9; rep from * around—18 sts in each rep between markers.

Rnd 29: *Yo, ssk, k2tog, yo, k1, yo, ssk, k2tog, yo, [ssk, yo] twice, k1, [yo, k2tog] twice; rep from *around.

Rnd 31: *Yo, ssk, k2tog, yo, (k1, yo, k1, yo, k1) all in next st, yo, ssk, k2tog, yo, ssk, yo, k1, sk2p, k1, yo, k2tog; rep from *around—20 sts in each rep between markers.

Rnd 33: *Yo, ssk, k2tog, yo, k5, yo, ssk, k2tog, yo, ssk, yo, sk2p, yo, k2tog; rep from * around—18 sts in each rep between markers.

Rnd 35: *Yo, ssk, k2tog, yo, [k1, yo] 5 times, ssk, k2tog, yo, ssk, k1, k2tog; rep from * around—20 sts in each rep between markers.

Rnd 37: *Yo, ssk, k2tog, yo, k9, yo, ssk, k2tog, yo, sk2p; rep from * around—18 sts in each rep between markers.

With size 3 needle, rep Rnds 18–37.

With size 5 needle, rep Rnds 18–29.

Next rnd: Knit.

Next rnd: *Insert crochet hook into each of next 3 sts and remove sts from knitting needle (*see Fig. 1 on page 47*), yo and pull through all loops on hook, Fig. 2 (sc dec made), ch 7; rep from * around, join in first sc dec. Fasten off.

Finishing

With tapestry needle, run a gathering thread through cast-on edge of cover. With RS facing place cover over lamp shade; pull gathering thread ends until top edge fits top rim, and tie thread ends tog.

Spread fullness of evenly over shade. Glue cast-on edge to top rim of lamp shade. Cutting to fit, glue braided trim around top rim, covering top rim and cast-on edge of cover. Let glue dry.

Spreading fullness evenly around shade and stretching if necessary to fit, pin cover in place along lower edge. Glue bottom edge of cover to bottom rim of lamp shade. Let dry. Remove pins.

Cutting to fringe trim to fit and pinning in place as you go, glue fringe around lamp shade, covering bottom edge of cover. Let dry. Remove pins. ❖

Pineapple & Diamonds Table Runner

Continued from page 24

needle, replace marker on RH needle, sk2p, yo, k19, yo; rep from * around—24 sts in each rep.

Rnd 33: Removing markers as you come to them, *insert crochet hook into each of next 2 sts and remove sts from knitting needle (*see Fig. 1 on page 47*), yo and pull through all loops on hook, Fig. 2 (sc dec made), ch 9; ** insert crochet hook into each of next 3 sts and remove sts from knitting needle, yo and pull through all loops on hook, ch 9** rep from

** to ** around to other end of Runner; rep from * around, join with sl st in first sc. Fasten off.

Finishing

Spread knitted piece on blocking board, stretch to shape and pin the chain loops in place.

Spray knitted piece lightly with fabric stiffener or starch; let dry, then remove pins. ❖

E-mail: Customer_Service@whitebirches.com

Timeless Lace is published by DRG, 306 East Parr Road, Berne, IN 46711, telephone (260) 589-4000. Printed in USA. Copyright © 2009 DRG. All rights reserved. This publication may not be reproduced in part or in whole without written permission from the publisher.

RETAIL STORES: If you would like to carry this pattern book or any other DRG publications, call the Wholesale Department at Annie's Attic to set up a direct account: (903) 636-4303. Also, request a complete listing of publications available from DRG.

Every effort has been made to ensure that the instructions in this pattern book are complete and accurate. We cannot, however, take responsibility for human error, typographical mistakes or variations in individual work.

HOUSE of WHITE BIRCHES
PUBLISHERS SINCE 1947

STAFF

Editor: Jeanne Stauffer
Managing Editor: Dianne Schmidt
Technical Editor: Kathy Wesley
Copy Supervisor: Michelle Beck
Copy Editors: Amanda Ladig, Susanna Tobias
Technical Artist: Pam Gregory
Graphic Arts Supervisor: Ronda Bechinski
Graphic Artists: Erin Augsburger, Debby Keel
Art Director: Brad Snow
Assistant Art Director: Nick Pierce
Photography Supervisor: Tammy Christian
Photography: Matthew Owen
Photo Stylist: Tammy Steiner

ISBN: 978-1-59217-266-5

1 2 3 4 5 6 7 8 9

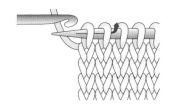

Fig. 1
Insert crochet hook into each of sts indicated,
removing sts from knitting needle.

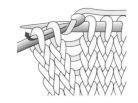

Fig. 2
Yarn over and pull yarn through
all loops on hook.

Knitting Needle Conversion Chart

U.S.	1	2	3	4	5	6	7	8	9	10	10½	11	13	15	17	19	35	50
Continental-mm	2.25	2.75	3.25	3.5	3.75	4	4.5	5	5.5	6	6.5	8	9	10	12.75	15	19	25

Inches into Millimetres & Centimetres

All measurements are rounded off slightly.

inches	mm	cm	inches	cm	inches	cm	inches	cm	inches	cm
⅛	3	0.3	3	7.5	13	33.0	26	66.0	39	99.0
¼	6	0.6	3½	9.0	14	35.5	27	68.5	40	101.5
⅜	10	1.0	4	10.0	15	38.0	28	71.0	41	104.0
½	13	1.3	4½	11.5	16	40.5	29	73.5	42	106.5
⅝	15	1.5	5	12.5	17	43.0	30	76.0	43	109.0
¾	20	2.0	5½	14	18	46.0	31	79.0	44	112.0
⅞	22	2.2	6	15.0	19	48.5	32	81.5	45	114.5
1	25	2.5	7	18.0	20	51.0	33	84.0	46	117.0
1¼	32	3.8	8	20.5	21	53.5	34	86.5	47	119.5
1½	38	3.8	9	23.0	22	56.0	35	89.0	48	122.0
1¾	45	4.5	10	25.5	23	58.5	36	91.5	49	124.5
2	50	5.0	11	28.0	24	61.0	37	94.0	50	127.0
2½	65	6.5	12	30.5	25	63.5	38	96.5		

Standard Abbreviations

[ ] work instructions within brackets as many times as directed

( ) work instructions within parentheses in the place directed

** repeat instructions following the asterisks as directed

* repeat instructions following the single asterisk as directed

" inch(es)

approx approximately

beg begin/beginning

CC contrasting color

ch chain stitch

cm centimeter(s)

cn cable needle

dec decrease/decreases/decreasing

dpn(s) double-pointed needle(s)

g gram

inc increase/increases/increasing

k knit

k2tog knit 2 stitches together

LH left hand

lp(s) loop(s)

m meter(s)

M1 make one stitch

MC main color

mm millimeter(s)

oz ounce(s)

p purl

pat(s) pattern(s)

p2tog purl 2 stitches together

psso pass slipped stitch over

p2sso pass 2 slipped stitches over

rem remain/remaining

rep repeat(s)

rev St st reverse stockinette stitch

RH right hand

rnd(s) rounds

RS right side

skp slip, knit, pass stitch over—one stitch decreased

sk2p slip 1, knit 2 together, pass slip stitch over the knit 2 together—2 stitches have been decreased

sl slip

sl 1k slip 1 knitwise

sl 1p slip 1 purlwise

sl st slip stitch(es)

ssk slip, slip, knit these 2 stitches together—a decrease

st(s) stitch(es)

St st stockinette stitch/stocking stitch

tbl through back loop(s)

tog together

WS wrong side

wyib with yarn in back

wyif with yarn in front

yd(s) yard(s)

yfwd yarn forward

yo yarn over

HOUSE of White Birches, Berne, Indiana 46711   DRGnetwork.com

Photo Index